How to use our guide

- All the practical information, hints and tips that you will need before and during the trip start on page 104.

- For general background, see the sections The Land and the People, p. 6, and A Brief History, p. 14.

- All the sights to see are listed between pages 21 and 83. Our own choice of sights most highly recommended is pinpointed by the Berlitz traveller symbol.

- Entertainment, nightlife and all other leisure activities are described between pages 84 and 95, while information on restaurants and cuisine is to be found on pages 96 to 103.

- Finally, there is an index at the back of the book, pp. 126–128.

Although we make every effort to ensure the accuracy of all the information in this book, changes occur incessantly. We cannot therefore take responsibility for facts, prices, addresses and circumstances in general that are constantly subject to alteration. Our guides are updated on a regular basis as we reprint, and we are always grateful to readers who let us know of any errors, changes or serious omissions they come across.

Text: Ken Bernstein
Photography: Eric Jaquier
Layout: Doris Haldemann
We're especially grateful to the Tourism Authority of Thailand for their help in the preparation of this book. We also wish to thank Tui Polasit and Claude Jotikasthira for their kind assistance.
Cartography: Falk-Verlag, Hamburg.

BERLITZ®

THAILAND

1988/1989 Edition

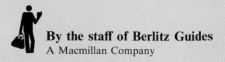

By the staff of Berlitz Guides
A Macmillan Company

Berlitz Trademark Reg. U.S. Patent Office and other countries.
Marca Registrada. Library of Congress Catalog Card No. 79-84594.
Printed in Switzerland by Weber S.A., Bienne.

4th Printing
(1981/1982 Edition)

Contents

 5

The Land and the People

With its dreamy tropical scenery, glittering temples and easy-going, beautiful people, Thailand delights every taste—aesthetic or eccentric, exotic or erotic. Because there's so much to see and do, you may barely find time for a swim.

The white sand and emerald seas lure many a long-distance sun-seeker when other continents are snowbound. But the balmy, palmy beaches are only the bright wrapping for the gifts within Thailand's borders: historic palaces, seething markets, archaeological parks, villages on stilts, jungle trails and forests where elephants earn their keep.

Bigger than Spain, but slightly smaller than France, Thailand has room enough for all the scenery anyone could want—with the possible exception of snowcapped mountains. Still the tallest peak, near Chiang Mai in the north, reaches a respectable height of about 8,500 feet. On the central plain around Bangkok, the world of rivers, canals and paddies is as flat and green as the proverbial billiard table. More than 70 per cent of the Thai population en-

gages in rice farming. So do several million water buffalo.

Thailand's climate, officially called Tropical Monsoon, is best between November and February. That's when relatively cool dry air rolls in from China, reducing Bangkok's temperatures from scorching to merely hot. And in the northern

hills you might be lucky enough to need a sweater after sundown. The south-west monsoon brings deluges, alternating with rainbows, from May to October.

Recent census figures indicate a population for Thailand of slightly more than 51 million. About one-tenth of the inhabitants are concentrated in Bangkok, the political and commercial capital and the only big city in a land of pleasant villages and small

Relaxed and smiling, Thais watch a professional snake-charmer's act.

towns. "Pleasant" is not the word for Bangkok's noise, air pollution and doomsday traffic jams, but the city has its charms. You can escape the heat on a long-tailed boat that skims through the canals, weaving between convoys of teak logs and rice barges plying the Chao Phya River. Ashore there are numerous enclaves of flowers, trees and peace, such as the spacious Buddhist monasteries topped with shining spires.

More than 90 per cent of Thais are Buddhists. The religion and philosophy of Buddhism permeate national life. Even in sophisticated, preoccupied Bangkok, women turn out in front of their houses soon after dawn to offer rice to the saffron-robed monks. And in Thailand, the calendar measures the years from 543 B.C., the beginning of the Buddhist era.

Buddhism is tolerant of other faiths. Christian missionaries have traditionally been the bearers of Western ideas and technology. Hinduism coexists with Buddhism, and not just among the local Indian colony; Brahmin priests still perform Thai royal functions. Buddhism also blends with animism. Notice the small shrines, rather like millionaire doll houses, next to homes, hotels and commercial buildings. There, food and flowers are offered to placate the spirits.

For those living in stilt-houses along the Mekong, the river is a highway, bathtub and fishpond.

Several million Chinese, mostly Buddhists, are well assimilated in Thailand. A smaller minority group—about a million Moslems—live mainly in the south, where they retain their own customs and the Malay language. In the north, hill tribesmen in semi-primitive societies choose to remain on the edge of national life.

Thais on the whole are a graceful, handsome, high-cheekboned people. They are relaxed but vigorous. They take a cool view of life, an amused detachment that goes a long way towards avoiding disputes. "Thailand" means "land of the free" and personal liberty has great significance. Unlike the rest of South-East Asia, Thailand was never colonized by a European power, so the people's attitude towards foreigners is untinged by historic resentment. They are proud of their past and their royalty. The constitutional monarchy plays a lively role in uniting the country.

To see Thailand you have to escape the metropolis and discover the provinces, where the pace is relaxed and *fa-*

Ornate details cover the sides of
10 *Bangkok's Temple of the Dawn.*

rangs (foreigners) still provoke friendly smiles—or even open-mouthed stares. You can get away by jet plane, express train or air-conditioned bus. Once you reach calmer climes, you'll enjoy the switch to more typically Thai transport—motorcycle-powered *tuk-tuks*, or even pedicabs, the man-propelled taxis that are slow but quiet.

You can go north for mountain scenery, tribal cultures and handicrafts, bountiful fruits and flowers—including the poppies of the infamous Golden Triangle. Go north-east for ancient Khmer ruins, protected deer and tigers, and the biggest banyan tree the spirits ever haunted. If you go south, be prepared for perfect beaches and boat trips amidst surreal islands. Closer to Bangkok, you can spend a day or weeks among the palaces and pagodas, gleaning archaeological insights into a thousand years of history and art. You can keep your distance in the presence of fearsome crocodiles or deadly snakes, or shake hands with the most mischievous free-roaming monkeys ever to steal bananas by the bunch.

Any list of Thailand's attractions must mention Bangkok's nightlife, which has achieved a worldwide reputation for its lusty, uncomplicated good humour. Anything, as they say, goes; but the bars and allied establishments primly close at midnight (except on Friday and Saturday nights). Quieter evenings may be spent watching temple dancers with eloquent hands acting out traditional stories to the tune of celestial music. Folklore and sports combine in Thai boxing, a ritual combat mobilizing fists, elbows, knees and bare feet. The shopping is exciting, too, whether in floating markets, vast bazaars or air-conditioned boutiques. The native food, with brilliant invention, presents startling contrasts of flavours. The Thais are fond of spicy hot dishes but the chefs take pity on frail foreigners. Delicious tropical fruits help put out the fire too.

For all their virtues, the Thais often perplex foreign visitors accustomed to Western notions of punctuality and efficiency. The Thais decline to be fanatical about productivity or deadlines; they work hard only if a job is interesting or, better yet, amusing. Something that amuses them greatly is gambling—the lottery, the horses, cockfights, even fishfights and a species of bullfight. They acknowledge no caste system, yet a sense of status governs many nuances of their human relations. Just when you come to the conclusion that women are relegated to a subservient role, you stumble upon a female tycoon or an all-girl bank where even the security guards are karate-keen women.

The sudden change of climate and culture may overwhelm you. The whole country may seem to be hiding behind a curtain of inscrutability. But if mystery means escapism, then Thailand should make the perfect holiday.

Taking a break from meditations, monks set off on afternoon stroll.

A Brief History

Thailand was inhabited thousands of years ago—but not by the Thais. They arrived from southern China fairly late in the game, probably in the 11th and 12th centuries. The history of the land is still being rewritten. Scholars are analyzing recent archaeological finds in north-east Thailand, the most interesting of them at the village of Ban Chiang. The relics there seem to prove the existence of stable Bronze Age communities more than 5,000 years ago—a jolt to conventional theories about the dawn of civilization.

What happened to the prehistoric people is not known. As for the Thais, their early history is obscure for several reasons. They were on the move; spiritual matters—and sheer survival—were more important than record-keeping; and whatever early documents did exist were destroyed by vengeful invaders in the 18th century.

The first notable king of the Thais, Mengrai the Great, built a prosperous and progressive society in what is now northern Thailand. He founded the towns of Chiang Rai and Chiang Mai in the late 13th cen-

tury. The temples which survive from that era show the important place Buddhism held in their society. The religion is said to have come from India, with additional influences from the Mon and Khmer peoples.

Mengrai ruled until the age of 80, when a lightning bolt

struck him. (Later kings died in even more bizarre ways. King Kamphoo's brief reign ended in 1345 when he was devoured by a crocodile. In modern times, Rama VIII, the older brother of the present king, was found shot dead in bed; this 1946 mystery has never been solved.)

Sukhothai

The first great age of Thai culture began under King Ramkamhaeng the Great, who ruled Sukhothai (founded in the 1230s) from about 1280 to

Melancholy mood amidst medieval monuments at sunset in Sukhothai.

1317. Ramkamhaeng attracted the technology, art and thought of China. India and Cambodia. He was responsible for the creation of the Thai alphabet. One of the earliest inscriptions describes his happy realm: "In the water there are fish, in the fields there is rice... Whoever wants to trade in elephants, so trades... Whoever wants to trade in silver and gold, so trades." In what might be interpreted as a preview of modern day "swinging Bangkok", the same manuscript says: "Whoever wants to make merry, does so."

At its peak under King Ramkamhaeng, Sukhothai began to slide downhill after his death. By the 15th century the city was a mere provincial town, and soon afterwards, it was abandoned.

Ayutthaya
Sukhothai had been eclipsed by the Kingdom of Ayutthaya, a high point in Thai history. Founded around 1350, Ayutthaya—which came to be known as Siam—eventually expanded into parts of what are now Laos, Burma, Kampuchea and Malaysia. The kingdom

Child hides in shadow of smiling statue of Buddha in old Ayutthaya.

also widened its cultural frontiers through contacts with the rest of the world. The contacts were practical as well as intellectual. Diplomatic relations with Portugal, inaugurated in the 16th century, brought Western guns and military tactics to the elephant-cavalry forces of Siam. The new hardware and ideas helped Ayutthaya to overcome rival armies.

Foreigners who reached Ayutthaya in the 17th century were astounded at the size and opulence of the Siamese capital. Estimates of its population range from 300,000 to 1,000,000, making Ayutthaya bigger than most European capitals of the day. And with its palaces and temples, canals and bridges, the city was charming as well as exotic.

European influence reached its zenith in the reign of King Narai (1657–88), who welcomed European diplomats, traders and missionaries. He also named a Greek, Constantine Phaulkon, as his minister of foreign trade. The influential European sparked bitter jealousies; when the king died, Phaulkon was arrested and executed.

Between the 15th and 18th centuries the Thais fought countless skirmishes, battles and wars against Burma. The **17** most fateful, four-year war ended in April 1767, when the Burmese captured Ayutthaya. They pillaged the capital and vandalized every evidence of Thai culture and art. The sack of Ayutthaya, a great national tragedy, still saddens the Thai consciousness.

One survivor of the calamity, the governor of Tak province, was able to rally the remnants of the Thai army to counterattack the Burmese occupation forces. He scored a tactical victory but by then Ayutthaya was only a ghost town. Taksin, as he was known, founded a new capital at Thon Buri, directly across the river from what is now Bangkok. Though his father was Chinese—and a commoner, at that—Taksin was crowned the Thai king. He ruled until 1782 when he was dethroned and executed on grounds of madness.

The Bangkok Period

The doomed Taksin was succeeded by his lifelong friend, General Phya Chakri, the great-great-grandson of the Thai ambassador to the court of Louis XIV at Versailles. General Chakri became King Rama I, named after the hero of the Thai national epic. He founded the present Chakri dynasty. His descendant, King Bhumibol Adulyadej, reigns today as Rama IX.

Because the palace was crowded between two monasteries in Thon Buri, the king decided to move to roomier— and more militarily defensible—terrain on the east bank of the river. So Bangkok became Thailand's fourth capital.

The biography of his son, Rama II, provides a statistical footnote to the state of court polygamy in the 19th century. The monarch sired 73 children by 38 mothers. Two of his sons became kings of Siam—Rama III and IV.

Rama III, who reigned from 1824 to 1851, reopened the country to Western influences after more than a century of xenophobia. During his era the first United States envoy arrived in Bangkok, followed by American missionaries, one of whom brought the first printing press with Thai type.

King Mongkut

The achievements of the forward-looking King Mongkut (Rama IV) are proudly recalled in Thailand. But abroad he is better known in a fictionalized version—*The King and I*. The film has never been released in Thailand on grounds that it shows disrespect to the monarchy. The original book, by a court tutor Anna Leonowens, scarcely hinted at Mongkut's sophistication. He was, in fact, better educated than the kings of Europe. He knew seven foreign languages, including Latin and English. In his reign for the first time commoners were permitted to set eyes on the king of Siam. He sent diplomats to England and France and wrote to Abraham Lincoln offering technical assistance during the American Civil War. The U.S. president declined the offer of a pair of elephants.

Mongkut's son, King Chulalongkorn (Rama V), presided over more drastic reforms. He abolished slavery and established schools, a museum, a national library and Siam's first post office. Literally as well as symbolically he led his country into the 20th century. Rama V died after a long, useful reign in 1910; he is still remembered with affection.

The World Wars

Siam's physical and philosophical remoteness from Europe came to an abrupt end in 1917. King Vajiravudh (Rama VI) sent troops to France to join the Allied cause in the First World War. One explanation for his sympathies: he had been educated at Cambridge and served for a time in the British army. After the war Siam joined the League of Nations.

One legacy of Rama VI was a name for every Thai. Before World War I, family names were not used in Siam. The king decreed that everyone should adopt one. To this day, Thais are known by their first names, while surnames are only used for more or less formal purposes.

A changing world caught up with Siam in 1932 when a constitutional monarchy was imposed. King Rama VII, last of the absolute rulers, acceded to the new constitution limiting his powers. But three years later, after a series of intrigues, revolts and coups d'état, he abdicated.

In an effort to regain territory they had been forced to cede to the French, the authorities of Siam (by then renamed Thailand) signed friendship pacts with the Japanese in 1940.

The following year Japanese troops landed in Thailand. And soon afterwards the Thais, considering resistance hopeless, entered World War II on the side of the Axis. The home front experienced drastically mixed feelings. Although Thailand was counted on the losing side, it was later invited to join the United Nations organi- **19** zation because of a legalistic loophole in the original declaration of war.

In the postwar years Thailand's foreign policy veered from active anti-communism as an American ally in the Indochina war to a determined attempt at neutrality. On the domestic scene, democratic experiments alternated with military dictatorships. The country bounced from coup to counter-coup, from student revolt and guerrilla insurgency to repression and reform. Few dare predict which way Thailand will go from here—not while the political cauldron of South-East Asia keeps bubbling.

Where to Go

Bangkok

Bangkok is full of fascinations—but rarely for the idle stroller. The great distances, and the heat, make it one of the world's least walkable cities. Aimless sauntering may produce nothing more memorable than a twisted ankle, for the walkways are chronically torn up.

The sensible way to get to know Bangkok is by guided tour aboard an air-conditioned car or coach. Travel agencies run several different half-day and full-day programmes, both general and specialized. After you've figured out the geography you can explore on your own, by taxi or bus. But walking is for the foolhardy.

Bangkok's Heart

In 1782 King Rama I established his capital on the bulging side of a bend in the Chao Phya River—for security reasons. With the river on his west and a moat to protect the eastern approaches, he didn't have to

Pop stars and traditional vendors' baskets coexist in modern Bangkok.

Calling All Farangs

Here are a few essential Thai words you'll hear and even begin to use:

Farang. Foreigner (but with no pejorative sense).

Klong. Canal.

Mai pen rai. The all-purpose "never mind" expression; say it instead of losing your temper, or all hope.

Samlor. Noisy motorized pedicab.

Sanuk. Fun.

Sarong. Woman's wrap-around garment; in the countryside men often wear something similar called *pakoma.*

Tuk-tuk. Noisy three- or four-wheeled minibus.

Wai. Prayer-like greeting with palms of hands together and head inclined.

Wat. A monastery or temple complex.

worry about surprise attack and could concentrate on building palaces and temples in what had been a nondescript fishing and trading village. The name of the new capital was Krungthep, meaning "city of angels". The Thais still call it that, but foreigners know the city as Bangkok.

The capital of Rama I, only a thin sliver of today's metropolis, is a fitting place to start exploring the art, architecture, religion and character of the Thai people.

Start your visit with the **Grand Palace,** a fabulous city within a city: opulent spires, gateways guarded by oriental "monsters", banquet halls, cloisters, monks resting beneath banyan trees... in a word, Siam. Royal, religious and government buildings crowd together inside a white-washed crenelated wall over a mile long. Enter through the Vised Chaisri Gate, on the north side of the compound,

Fantastic spires and statues mark central Bangkok's Grand Palace.

opposite the Pramane Ground. On weekends, admission is free, but the buildings are closed to the public. (Until a few years ago visitors were obliged to wear jackets and neckties, or long dresses, but the rules of formality have been relaxed. Modesty in dress is still enforced, however.)

The first four kings of the Chakri dynasty lived their entire reigns within these walls. Each added new buildings in evolving styles, from traditional Thai with steeply sloping tile roofs to neo-classical European structures.

A pair of 200-year-old lions—Chinese stone sculp-

tures—stand fiercely before the gate leading to the **Audience Hall of Dusit Maha Prasad.** These flamboyant statues are said to have reached Bangkok as ballast on Chinese junks which came to fetch Thai rice. The Dusit Hall itself is a classical Thai palace with an X-shaped floor plan and roofs rising in four tiers, topped by a slim gilt spire. Just alongside, a beautifully carved miniature **pavilion** served as the royal changing room on ceremonial occasions.

Amidst all the "King and I" architecture, one palace stands out with wonderful incongruity. The internationally minded King Rama V built the Chakri Maha Prasad **Throne Hall** in 1876 as a fusion of East and West. What might have been a European parliament building is surmounted by Thai roofs and towers; European street lights and well-ordered gardens complete the ensemble. On the edge of the square is another royal changing pavilion with landings from which the king could mount his elephant or a hand-carried litter *(palanquin)*. Beyond this,

In Lakmuang shrine, a traditional dance gives thanks for blessings; outside, exotic foodstuffs galore.

the **Audience Hall of Amarindra** is furnished in total splendour. It is still used for royal ceremonies.

Among all the other signs of affluence is a separate, modestly titled Coin Museum. Within glass cases in two jail-like enclaves are displayed crown jewels, gold swords and tea sets (also gold). The security measures would pose an intriguing challenge for any master criminal.

So much for the temporal. **Wat Phra Keo,** the Royal Chapel of the Grand Palace complex, contains one of Thailand's most venerated religious images, the **Emerald Buddha**

(actually made of jasper). Dramatic light effects enhance the impression of awe. But the statue, enshrined in an elevated golden altar, is only about two feet high. Photography is forbidden inside the Royal Chapel. You'll be reminded to leave your shoes outside, and as you sit on the floor taking in the grandeur of the scene, make sure (here, as in all temples) that the bottom of your feet do not point towards the altar.

Across the road from all the royal pomp is a small temple-like structure you might easily overlook. It houses the **Lakmuang** or foundation stone of Bangkok, supposedly placed

there by Rama I. The local people, who attribute great powers to the resident spirits, surround the pillar with flowers, candles and smoking incense sticks. Thankful for favours granted, the faithful engage Thai dancers (always on call) to go through the traditional paces. On the fringes,

Market Medley
The colour and activity of a Thai market is worth going a long way to see. There seems no end to the variety of goods on sale at certain: live chicken and ducks, more species of garlic and pepper than you knew existed, shoes, mouse-traps, ceremonial fighting swords, jeans, white mice (and mice dyed pink, green or yellow), fluffy puppies and even Siamese cats. Bangkok has no shortage of ordinary cats, but blue-eyed Siamese, of regal disposition, are more rare here than in the parlours of Europe and America.

people sell food, amulets and lottery tickets. Outside, children ask passers-by to buy birds—not to keep, but to release from cages as an act of Buddhist piety. Nothing about this whole startling scene is staged for tourists; in fact, this is one place a *farang* is simply ignored.

The **Pramane Ground,** also known as Sanam Luang, is an immense open space suitable for royal funerals. It used to be the scene of a fantastic weekend market that has moved

Squadron of fighting kites awaits next combat on Pramane Ground.

What's Wat

Thailand's thousands of wats—Buddhist monasteries or temple compounds—have a vocabulary all their own. Here's a brief rundown of the most common architectural terms:

Bot: Temple where religious rites are held.

Chedi: Bell-like dome, often containing holy relics.

Prang: Cylinder with rounded top, pointing up like a finger.

Stupa: Tower or pagoda, often burial site.

Viharn or *wihan:* Preaching or worship hall.

out of town centre to Chatuchak Park (see p. 88).

Facing the west side of the Pramane Ground is a long row of official buildings of architectural, cultural or historical importance. These include two universities, a temple, the national library, museum and theatre. The **National Museum,** which may be the largest in South-East Asia, fills an 18th-century palace and supplementary buildings old and new. Thailand's artistic treasures, from prehistoric to contemporary, are on show—sculpture, textiles, jewellery, weapons, thrones. Details on page 40.

Six Great Wats

Metropolitan Bangkok counts dozens of important wats—monasteries or temple complexes. For the visitor in a hurry, we've narrowed the field to six unforgettable ones.

Bangkok's best-known landmark, **Wat Arun** (the Temple of Dawn), stands on the opposite bank of the Chao Phya River in Thon Buri—but it's only a minute or two away by ferry. Photographers can't resist the central tower, taller than a 20-storey building, looming like an elongated Aztec pyramid. Four similar lesser towers surround the central *prang.* All are made of brick but covered with stucco planted with chips of ceramic that flash in the sunlight. You can climb halfway up the side of the central structure. The steps are steep, but the view of the river and the royal compound opposite justifies the effort.

Wat Pho, the oldest monastery in Bangkok, founded in the 16th century when the future capital was but a village, is known for its stupendous gilt **Reclining Buddha.** Nearly 50 feet high and 150 feet long, it

Something's always happening at Wat Pho, even Thai boxing tune-up.

reaches right up to the roof of the temple.

Home to several hundred priests, Wat Pho is also Bangkok's biggest monastery and contains many other admirable works of art. The marble bas-reliefs, rescued from the ruins of Ayutthaya, make coveted temple rubbings. Unfortunately, a brisk commercial undertone somewhat mars the monastery's tranquillity: at the exit, tourists are accosted by postcard salesmen and food hawkers, but the courtyard of the temple proper is quiet and peaceful enough.

Walls within walls protect **Wat Suthat** monastery on the square of the Giant Swing, a tall teak structure painted bright red. In days gone by, death-defying swingers used to show off their acrobatic skill during the annual Brahmin

Pensive girl at Wat Pho; right: Golden Buddha of Wat Trimitr.

harvest festival. In the elegant *viharn* of Wat Suthat you'll find an immense and beautiful seated Buddha. Outside, at the four corners of the building, stand graceful bronze horses. This neighbourhood is full of shops specializing in religious goods—Buddha statues of all sizes as well as accessories for Buddhist and Hindu devotions.

Wat Saket, better known as the Golden Mount, really stands out. Atop Bangkok's only hill—artificial, at that— the temple is surmounted by a big gold *chedi*. Steps spiralling up the reinforced sides of the mount lead to a viewing platform. Take a map along so you can identify the palaces and temples spread around the terrain below. The faithful make the climb less for the view than for the shrine containing relics of the Buddha. They were given to King Rama V by Lord Curzon, then Viceroy of India.

Midway between the hurly-burly of the National Assembly and the Royal Turf Club, you'll find **Wat Benchamabophit,** the **Marble Temple,** a haven of grace and calm. It was built in 1899 by order of Rama V, the world-travelled reformer king who encouraged all the arts in Thailand. The temple's elegant lines are accentuated by white Carrara marble imported from

Italy for the project, golden Chinese tiles cover the intricately interlaced roofs, and a pair of huge marble lions guard the entrance to the *bot.* Flowering trees, lotus ponds and clipped lawns add to the cool attraction of the scene.

The renowned **Golden Buddha** may be found in a utilitarian chapel to the left of the main temple of **Wat Traimit** on the edge of Bangkok's Chinatown. The brilliant gold of the seated Buddha reflects **31** the spotlights thoughtfully provided for photographers. In 1953 an undistinguished but heavy Buddha image was being moved by crane when the hook broke. The cracked stucco revealed solid gold within. Presumably the Golden Buddha, 700 or 800 years old, had been disguised to protect it from Burmese invaders. Even if the statue weren't old and artistically pleasing, the 5½ tons of solid gold would still evoke admiration.

Bangkok Afloat

The most popular tourist excursion in Bangkok, the **Floating Market** Tour, explores the major *klongs* (canals) to the west of the city. The tour starts early in the morning to catch the vendors on their rounds, paddling past the canal-front houses with specialized cargo: fruit or vegetables or household necessities. Once the citizens of Thon Buri realized how interesting their way of life was to the *farangs*, commercialization was inevitable. Still, it's a fast way to see life along the waterways, and the boat people, mostly women in outsized straw hats, are a photographer's delight.

The morning tour always includes a ride on the Chao Phya River and a look at the **royal barges** in their shed in Klong Bangkok Noi. All the ceremonial craft are dreamboats—other-worldly vessels, low and long with elaborate red and gold decorations and fanciful prows. The monarch's own boat is propelled by 50 oarsmen.

You can see the canals on your own by taking the local shuttle boats, the long-tailed *hang yaos.* These narrow, shallow-draught 30-footers, powered by noisy truck engines, have the propellor on the end of a long swivelling drive shaft—hence the name, "longtailed" boats. You can also hire your own *hang yao* by the hour—but, as in the taxi business, be sure to agree on a price in advance.

On the quiet canals reachable only by these boats you'll see how much of the city's life still revolves around the waterways: crowded old stilt houses alongside handsome new homes with gardens and fountains; factories and shipyards; floating vegetable markets and snack bars being paddled past shy maidens bathing in the muddy water; children in their

32

Avoiding Bangkok's hopeless road traffic, boats of "floating market" move food through canal network.

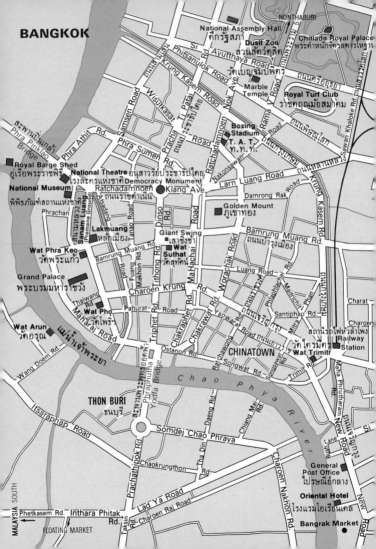

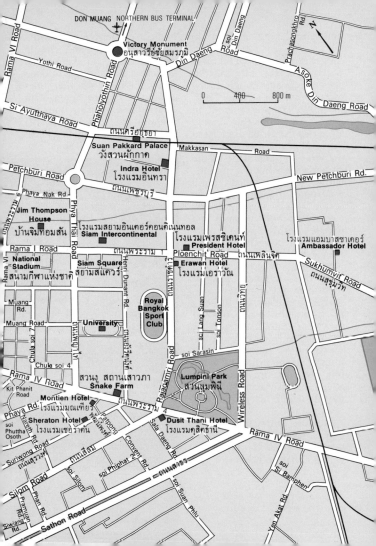

DON MUANG NORTHERN BUS TERMINAL

Victory Monument
อนุสาวรีย์ชัยสมรภูมิ

Rama VI Road

Yothi Road

Phaholyothin Road

Din Daeng Road

Prachasongkhro Road

soi Din Daeng Road

Asoke Din Daeng Road

Si Ayutthaya Road

0   400   800 m

ถนนครีอยุธยา

Suan Pakkard Palace
วังสวนผักกาด

Makkasan   Road

Petchburi Road

Indra Hotel
โรงแรมอินทรา

ถนนเพชรบุรี

New Petchburi Rd.

Phaya Nak Rd.

Jim Thompson House
บ้านจิมทอมสัน

Phya Thai Road

โรงแรมสยามอินเตอร์คอนติเนนทอล
Siam Intercontinental

ถนนพระราม

โรงแรมเพรสซิเดนท์
President Hotel

Ploenchit Road

ถนนเพลินจิต

โรงแรมแอมบาสซาเดอร์
Ambassador Hotel

Rama I Road

National Stadium
สนามกีฬาแห่งชาติ

Rama VI

Siam Square
สยามสแควร์

Henri Dunant Rd.

Erawan Hotel
โรงแรมเอราวัณ

Sukhumvit Road
ถนนสุขุมวิท

Muang Rd.

Muang Road

Royal Bangkok Sport Club

soi Lang Suan

soi Tonson

ถนนวิทยุ

University

Chula soi 7

Chula soi 4

ถนนพญาไท

ถนนอังรีดูนังต์

soi Sarasin

Rama IV Road

สวนงู สถานเสาวภา
Snake Farm

ถนนพระราม

Lumpini Park
สวนลุมพินี

Wireless Road

Kit Phanit Road

Montien Hotel
โรงแรมมณเฑียร

Phya Rd.

Patpong

Rajadamri Road

4

Dusit Thani Hotel
โรงแรมดุสิตธานี

soi Phuttha Osoth

Sheraton Hotel
โรงแรมเชอราตัน

Sala Daeng Rd.

Rama IV Road

Suriwong Road
ถนนสุริวงศ์

Convent Rd.

ถนนสีลม

ถนนสาทร

soi Si Bamphen

Silom Road

soi Silom

soi Phiphat

soi Suan Phlu

Pramuan Rd.

Phan Rd.

Siwiang Rd.

Sathon Road

Yen Akat Rd.

uniforms taking a boat to school.

A cheap way to see the river is aboard a river bus, called a *baht* boat, even though it now costs several times that. These fast, noisy boats take about an hour to go from the landing alongside the Oriental Hotel to the northern terminus at Nonthaburi. The character of the city changes by the minute. Crowded warehouses and government buildings give way to old shacks surrounded by mangroves and palms. You mingle with scows heavily laden with coconuts, tankers, navy destroyers, water-taxis, houseboats, barges; you see Bangkok's temples, palaces, mansions and bridges. Passengers get on and off all along the route, on both sides of the river—commuters, soldiers, students, secretaries, saffronrobed monks and white-robed nuns. If you go to the end of the line, Nonthaburi, you'll discover a more relaxed world than Bangkok; they even have pedicabs.

Among other water-borne excursions offered by travel agencies: a sunset tour of the canals aboard a converted rice barge, a dinner cruise on a luxurious river barge and trips up the great river to Bang Pa-in aboard the air-conditioned *Oriental Queen*. Another longdistance excursion begins with a two-hour drive from Bangkok to Damnoen Saduak, where the floating market retains a lot of authenticity (see p. 43).

Billboards promoting films are an art form; buses go in slow motion.

Centres of Town

Bangkok is a horizontal city. Except for a very few, modest efforts at skyscraping, the metropolis remains nearly as flat as the rice fields it took over—mile after mile of two, three or four-storey buildings. Because it is so decentralized, Bangkok has no real centre, no pre-eminent neighbourhood. Instead, several districts, widely dispersed, call for attention.

Between the neo-classical National Assembly building and the Democracy Monument runs a wide, leafy boulevard, **Ratchadamnoen Nok.** Bangkok's version of the Champs-Elysées is lined with govern-

ment office buildings, often with steep traditional roofs. For tourists the boulevard has two attractions: the Ratchadamnoen Boxing Stadium and, next door, the headquarters of the Tourism Authority of Thailand. Here you can pick up brochures and maps, ask questions and make reservations for resort hotels operated by T.A.T.

One of the original shopping centres of Bangkok is the **New Road** district (also known as Charoen Krung Road) around the General Post Office, an area still well supplied with souvenir shops and "instant" tailors. Between the road and the river here you'll find several embassies and the century-old Oriental Hotel, distinguished as the haunt of literary celebrities like Joseph Conrad, Noel Coward and Somerset Maugham. A few streets to the south lies the lively Bangrak market, always full of fish, flowers, fruit and fun.

In Bangkok's **Chinatown,** about midway between the New Road area and the Pramane Ground, every shopfront means a new discovery: snake wine or gold pendants, paper dragons or lottery tickets. The district covers a lot of ground, but the main crossroads is at Yaowarat and Ratchawong roads. The most interesting

shops fill the narrow lanes between Yaowarat and the river. And, naturally, the area is lavishly supplied with noodle shops and Chinese snack-bars.

Several important centres of activity are located on Rama I Road, which changes its name twice as it proceeds east—to Ploenchit Road and then, for a long stretch, to Sukhumvit Road.

The **Siam Square** area has cinemas, restaurants, shops and Siam Centre, a big shopping and office block. Alongside, in its own park the Siam Intercontinental Hotel achieves architectural distinction. It also has its own private zoo.

At the next major intersection, by the Erawan Hotel, you may be unnerved to find that not only most bus passengers but most drivers as well raise hands in the *wai* gesture as they pass by. They are not paying homage to any dignitary staying at the government-run hotel but to a simple shrine in the grounds. Many small miracles are attributed to the **Erawan Shrine,** enclosing a golden image of a Hindu god. The street corner is crowded with insistent

On Chao Phya River, stevedores walk the plank with 200-lb. sacks.

urchins peddling flowers and incense sticks.

Farther east, across the railway tracks which lead all the way to Chiang Mai, the road has changed its name to **Sukhumvit.** Here begins a rambling shopping, entertainment and residential area. The numbers identifying the *soi*'s, side-streets, seem to rise indefinitely before you eventually reach the end of town and the highway to Pattaya.

A final centre of town to contend with runs along two parallel roads, Silom and Suriwong. The biggest landmark is the spire of the Dusit Thani Hotel. The financial and commercial

tone of the area is over-shadowed by the notoriety of two of its small streets, **Patpong** I and II. From Munich to Melbourne the name Patpong evokes the image of go-go bars and massage parlours. The streets are privately owned, by the industrialist Patana Pongpanit, hence Patpong for short. As a sociological phenomenon, Patpong ought to be seen if not sampled.

Museums

The national treasures of Thailand, displayed in the **National Museum,** are so extensive and exotic that the visitor may be overwhelmed. Try to get there at 9.30 a. m. for one of the free guided tours which unravel some of the mystery (ask at your hotel which days it is given in English). Next best idea is to buy an explanatory booklet, with a map of the grounds, on sale at the entrance hall. The museum closes on Mondays, Fridays and holidays; on Sundays it's free. (See also HOURS in Blueprint.)

The earliest works of art are among the most interesting of all. They come from excavations at Ban Chiang, in north-eastern Thailand—pots and jars with bold fingerprint-shaped whorl designs. The

haunting patterns are curiously modern, yet the pottery is probably 5,000 years old.

Thai culture is divided into several major periods, beginning with the Dvaravati (6th to 11th century A. D.) and moving with the political power to Sukhothai, then Ayutthaya, and ultimately to Bangkok (late 18th-century to present-day art is also known as Ratanakosin). As you go through the rooms chronologically, you can see the changes in the portrayal of the Buddha, the overriding theme of Thai art.

The museum has many other departments full of the most unexpected items: ancient cannon, 19th-century Thai typewriters, a full-scale model elephant fitted out for battle, historic royal regalia, thrones, litters and a hangar full of ark-sized royal funeral cars of unparalleled grandeur.

Besides the insight offered into Thai history and art, a visit to the National Museum gives you a chance to watch groups of schoolchildren, soldiers and monks earnestly studying their national heritage.

A museum on a more manageable scale, the **Suan Pakkard Palace** consists of fine old wooden stilt houses filled with great Thai art. On the lawns a gruff but friendly pelican holds court. At the bottom of the impeccable garden is a precious building, the Lacquer Pavilion, said to be the only house of its type to survive the sack of Ayutthaya in 1767. A gift to the owner Princess Chumbot from her late husband, the pavilion was bought in 1959 and reconstructed here. Some inside walls are covered with exquisite paintings in gold leaf on black lacquer showing episodes of the life of the Buddha and of the national legend, the Ramakien. Suan Pakkard (which means lettuce garden) is open daily except Sunday.

Jim Thompson's house, the glorious, cluttered home of a great collector, is full of works of Oriental art, mostly Thai, mostly priceless. Guided tours in English or French explain the significance of the outstanding sculptures, paintings and ceramics, as well as the architectural aspects of the composite Thai teak house reassembled to his design.

The story of Jim Thompson is as intriguing as his taste in art. A New York architect, he came to South-East Asia during World War II as a secret agent. After the war he settled in Bangkok, where he converted the Thai silk industry from a primitive craft into international big business. In 1967, on a holiday in neighbouring Malaysia, he vanished. The mystery is unsolved. No trace of Thompson has ever been found, but his monument—"the house on the *klong*"—remains as he left it. Open Monday to Friday.

If you'd like to pay a visit to the silk company afterwards, have the taxi wait for you. Otherwise you may fall into the hands of touts who misdirect tourists to competing and sometimes fairly seedy shops all over town.

Diversions

Other Bangkok attractions include the trio below:

Siam Park. This Western-style amusement park in the Minburi suburb has everything from water slides and free-form pool to a mock Thai village and crafts bazaar.

Snake farm. This is the stuff of nightmares—but at least it's all in a good cause. The Thai Red Cross Society provides snakebite serum for much of the world. To manufacture the serum the society must maintain a steady source of venom, hence the crowds of slithering specimens on view. Hypnotically patterned cobras, gaily striped banded kraits, spotted vipers and other killers are milked for humanity—and the edification of tourists—every morning at 11. The farm, at Rama IV and Henri Dunant roads, is closed on holidays.

Dusit Zoo. Elephants beg bananas, deer beg pineapple, and jumbo fish in the lake dote on bread and popcorn tossed their way by charitable patrons. If all this gives you sympathetic pangs, there are plenty of snack stalls for humans, too. Aside from the animals and an admirably landscaped aviary, the zoo is probably the best vantage point in Bangkok for watching Thai children and their parents having fun. Open every day.

Bangkok Daytrips

Westwards

All the travel agencies run half-day package tours to the **Rose Garden,** a private resort 32 kilometres west of Bangkok. Actually, the roses are only a small part of the 50 acres of heavenly tropical gardens. Every afternoon a Thai Village Cultural Show is staged, offering a comprehensive introduction to Thai music, dance and traditional sports. They even simulate a wedding ceremony. The side-shows are engrossing, as well: craftswomen at work making umbrellas, pottery and

silk cloth. For kicks, you can take a ride on an elephant and even be photographed all wrapped up in a monstrously long but guaranteed "tame" python.

In Thailand, temples and pagodas are as much a part of the landscape as are castles in Spain or windmills in Holland. But **Nakhon Pathom** has a golden spire that stands out for miles around. The **Phra Pathom** *chedi*, resembling an overturned bowl capped with an ice-cream cone, holds the title of the tallest Buddhist monument in Thailand. The top of its spire is 395 feet above the ground.

In the middle of the 19th century King Mongkut ordered this *chedi* built atop the ruins of an ancient temple—possibly dating back more than 1,000 years—to which he had made a pilgrimage as a monk. The area had been abandoned to the jungle. Mongkut's son, Rama V, continued the project, installing the towering gold Buddha at the top of a dramatic marble staircase. The spire was raised in 1870.

A lesser feature of Nakhon Pathom, 58 kilometres west of Bangkok, is Sanam Chan Palace. This modern structure reproduces Thai traditional style except for an English Tudor building which was used as a setting for Shakespeare plays. Note, too, the statue of a dog named Yalay. He was greatly mourned by King Rama VI after allegedly being poisoned by jealous courtiers.

The canal network of **Damnoen Saduak,** a two-hour drive south-west of Bangkok, may seem like a long way to go to see another floating market. But the scene is less commercialized than in Bangkok. The sightseers—1,000 a day—descend from their coaches and cram into long, skinny motorboats

Animals at Work

In the endless green paddies of Thailand, water buffalo are as common a sight as the peasant women in their long-sleeved shirts and lampshade hats. The ungainly cattle, happy as children to wallow in mud, till the rice fields by the million.

Up-country in the timber zone, elephants are trained to haul heavy logs. They have a limited carrying capacity but plenty of power for pulling.

Even monkeys are put to work. A plantation in Thailand's southern peninsula employs trained monkeys to climb to the top of the tallest palms and, on direction, dislodge the ripest coconuts. Nimble and unafraid of heights, they work for peanuts.

or a high-speed journey through unspoiled canals. The area is a tropical Venice with palms and stilt houses. At the intersection of two main canals, throngs of shallow-draught canoes converge to sell their goods—fragrant watermelon and pineapple, spring onions and corn on the cob. When the tourists debark for a dockside view at this nautical traffic jam, smiling but sometimes pushy salesmen go to work peddling souvenirs, clothing and refreshments. It's hard to resist a three-year-old banana vendor

With trains a rarity, motorcyclist uses tragedy-scarred Kwai bridge.

when she clutches your hand and smiles into your eyes.

Some excursions include a visit to a nearby snake sideshow at which barefoot handlers show their courage and expertise. They also put a cobra and a mongoose together in the same cage to demonstrate the classical encounter between

these bizarre enem. mongoose quickly prc fatal advantage.

The name of the **River K** conjures up nearly as muc dread as that of the Styx. The novel by Pierre Boulle, and the film based on it, recounted the agony of the prisoners of war who built the now famous bridge. (Actually, there were three bridges; poetic license combined them.) But there is nothing fictional about the war cemeteries of **Kanchanaburi** (122 km. north-west of Bangkok): more than 8,000 graves of British, Dutch, Australian, Malayan, Indian, New Zealand, Canadian and Burmese prisoners and conscripts who, together with nearly 60,000 civilians, died during the construction of the Burma–Siam Railway. The inscriptions on the gravestones are as simple and moving as tragic poems.

The bridge itself, a particularly ungraceful iron span restored after the war, is still in use a couple of times a day. You can walk across the bridge, as the local folk do; in the unlikely event that a train appears, duck into one of the recessed escape platforms. Railway buffs can hardly resist the chance to ride these rails; organized tours exist for those who are dubious about reading a Thai timetable. **45**

…museum on the bank …ultry river gives insight …he everyday life of the …oners who built the "death …ilway". Set up in bamboo huts of the type used in the prison camps, the museum documents Japanese atrocities with photographs, paintings and relics. It also reveals the ingenuity of the prisoners in surviving great hardships, and the sympathy and help the local Thai population secretly offered the inmates.

North-west of Kanchanaburi, in the midst of absolute wilderness, adventurous businessmen have established bases for tourists who want to explore the jungle. One hotel, alongside the river, coddles its guests with air-conditioning and a swimming pool. A couple of others, slightly more spartan, are built on bamboo rafts floating in the stream. Excursions to caves, waterfalls and native villages can be arranged from these advance camps.

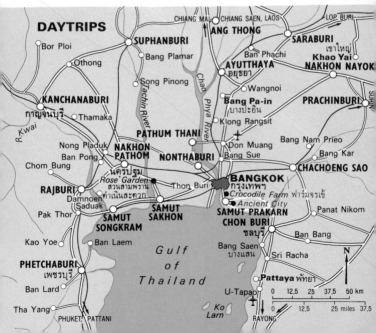

DAYTRIPS

CHIANG MAI · CHIANG SAEN, LAOS · LOP BURI

ANG THONG

Bor Ploi
SUPHANBURI
SARABURI
เขาใหญ่
Ban Phachi
Khao Yai
AYUTTHAYA
อยุธยา
NAKHON NAYOK
Othong
Bang Plamar
Song Pinong
Wangnoi
Bang Pa-in
บางปะอิน
PRACHINBURI
KANCHANABURI
กาญจนบุรี
Thamaka
Tachin River
Chao Phya River
Klong Rangsit
Bang Nam Prieo
R. Kwai
PATHUM THANI
Don Muang
Nong Pladuk
NAKHON
PATHOM
Bang Kar
Ban Pong
NONTHABURI
Bang Sue
Chom Bung
นครปฐม
CHACHOENGSAO
Rose Garden
สวนสามพราน
Thon Buri
BANGKOK
กรุงเทพฯ
RAJBURI
Crocodile Farm ฟาร์มจรเข้
Damnoen
Saduak
ดำเนินสะดวก
Ancient City
Panat Nikom
SAMUT
SAKHON
SAMUT PRAKARN
Pak Thor
CHON BURI
ชลบุรี
SAMUT
SONGKRAM
Ban Bang
Kao Yoe
Ban Laem
Gulf
Bang Saen
บางแสน
Sri Racha
PHETCHABURI
เพชรบุรี
of
Thailand
Ban Lard
Pattaya พัทยา
U-Tapao
0   12,5   25   37,5   50 km
Tha Yang
Ko
Larn
0   12,5   25 miles 37,5
PHUKET, PATTANI
RAYONG
N

Northwards

The royal estate of **Bang Pa-in**, about 60 kilometres north of Bangkok, was the weekend hide-away of the kings of Thailand when their capital was just up the river at Ayutthaya. The siege and sack of Ayutthaya by the Burmese in 1767 ended that bucolic era, but the charm of the ponds and palaces of Bang Pa-in remains.

You can get there by train, car or ferryboat. Most tourists choose the convenience and comfort of the *Oriental Queen*, a fast, air-conditioned cruiser which makes the run every day of the week. Heading up the Chao Phya River from Bangkok, the Queen passes houseboats, trains of low-slung barges and rafts of logs being manœuvred to market; and, ashore, coconut palms and lonely betel palms, stilt houses, temples, and a riverside monastery, Wat Pai Lom, which thousands of cranes have inexplicably chosen as their home.

Bang Pa-in's outstanding delight is a typically Thai pavilion with many-tiered, spiked roofs and a slender spire—all reflected in the shimmering lake which surrounds it. Another pavilion built in classical Chinese style is filled with lavish gifts to the Thai kings from China. Then there is an odd red-and-yellow striped building, reminiscent of a land-locked lighthouse.

The *Oriental Queen* excursions continue by coach to the city of **Ayutthaya** (86 km. north of Bangkok), from which the kingdom was ruled for four prosperous centuries. Sheep graze here amidst the ruins of a great capital. You can climb the steps of a red-brick *prang* to look over the immensity of the ancient city, laid waste by merciless invaders. Or hide in the shade of a solitary wall and let your imagination re-create the opulence of the era. With dozens of distinctive buildings and remains worth visiting, you'll be hard-pressed to see Ayutthaya in one day.

Guided tours often begin at **Viharn Phra Mongkol Borit,** a modern construction around what's said to be the biggest bronze Buddha statue in Thailand, four or five centuries old. Souvenir stalls in this part of the old city sell alleged antique Chinese pottery and Ayuttaya earthenware—or shards of it —from the golden age. Many of these relics are recovered by helmeted divers who scour the bottom of the nearby river. The supply seems almost limitless, so the prices ought to be

Ruins recall Ayutthaya's greatness; kids wallop Ancient City's bells.

reasonable—if you know how to bargain.

Wat Phra Ram is a gracefully designed 14th-century building amidst reflecting pools. The cloister is lined with stone Buddha images.

For an overview of the art of the age of Ayutthaya, visit the **Chao Sam Phraya Museum,** stocked with the best statues discovered in the ruins. There are bronze Buddhas of great beauty dating from the 13th and 14th centuries; 17th- and 18th-century door panels carved with religious or tra-

ditional or flower designs; and a great hoard of 15th-century gold jewellery.

Many treasures—of gold, crystal and precious stones— were unearthed from the 14th-century *prang* of **Wat Mahathat.** The outlines of its courtyards and galleries can still be discerned.

Next door. **Wat Rachaburana** was built in the 15th century around the tombs of Prince Ay and Prince Yi, brothers who slew each other in a tragic battle on elephant- back. Rare frescoes remain in the crypt, but thieves carried off the portable antiquities years ago.

A few miles out of town you can see the **kraal** used over the centuries for the mobilization and training of royal elephants. Wild elephants were lured into the stockade through a one-way entrance with tank trap.

Ayutthaya's presumed invulnerability was based on its layout—in effect, an artificial island protected by three rivers and a canal. The theory failed to hold back the Burmese invaders, but the ground plan remains impressive. You'll appreciate it more if you circumnavigate ancient Ayutthaya in a long-tailed boat. The landing stage is near Chandrakasem Palace.

South-Eastwards

To see Ayutthaya palaces and shrines as they looked before the plunder of 1767, visit **Ancient City,** 33 kilometres southeast of Bangkok. It's claimed to be the world's largest outdoor museum. What the Rose Garden, west of Bangkok, does for Thai culture, Ancient City attempts in the realm of Thai architecture. Covering approximately 200 acres laid out in the shape of the map of Thailand, Ancient City re-creates the greatest buildings in the country in full-size or slightly reduced scale. The reconstitution of the Ayutthaya structures was based on studies of **49** paintings, carvings, documents and the ruins themselves. The park is big and varied enough to keep children engrossed, and if not, they'll enjoy the monkeys, elephants and exotic birds. Note that the sign on one of the monkey bungalows reads, in Thai only: "Danger! Do not touch!"

Travel agencies run half-day outings to Ancient City, or you can go yourself any day of the week.

More superlatives: **Crocodile Farm** (25 km. south-east of Bangkok at Samut Prakarn) is billed as the world's largest establishment of its type. At last census its crocodile population numbered 50,000, from near and far. The "farm" serves two ends. First, it preserves endangered species of reptiles, while educating and amusing the public with a bizarre sort of zoo. On a more practical plane, the management makes a tidy profit from the export of crocodile meat and skins. You can't buy a crocburger on the premises but they do sell handbags, wallets, belts and even stuffed crocodiles. Several times a day a handler wrestles and otherwise dominates several of the big fellows for the tourists. Travel agencies in Bangkok run half-day tours, or you can go yourself.

Pattaya

Thailand's best-known, most successful beach resort may come as a shock. After a two-hour ride from Bangkok through flat, frankly uninspiring countryside, you're suddenly toppled into the midst of a go-go, fun-and-sun whirl on the alluring shore of the Gulf of Thailand. Everything in Pattaya is out in the tropical open air—sea sports, restaurants, hawkers, even somewhat sinful drinking establishments. There is no alternative to abandoning city clothes and manners and joining the rush to relax.

The mystery is why it took the world so long to discover the pleasures of these miles of palm-lined beaches. King Taksin set up camp in the vicinity, very briefly, 200 years ago but failed to give the seashore a second thought. Nothing more of consequence happened to the fishing village until 1961, when the first American servicemen arrived for what became known as "R & R"—rest and relaxation. The Thais eventually saw the possibilities and Pattaya evolved into a full-fledged international resort. Happily, it's still a fishing village as well. While the nightlife crowd catches up on its sleep, you can prowl the wharves at breakfast time and watch the fishermen unloading a bounty of seafood.

The bulk of the tourist traffic reaches Pattaya by bus from Bangkok. Half a dozen companies run luxury coaches several times a day. Fares are cheap, considering the distance (150 km.) and the wear-and-tear on the drivers—the traffic is always unnervingly undisciplined. Convenient train service also operates between Bangkok's airport and the resort. Thai Airways schedules connecting flights from Bangkok to U-Tapao airport, near Pattaya. And plans are under way for a hydrofoil service linking Bangkok and Pattaya by river and sea.

More than 8,000 hotel rooms or bungalows in Pattaya are officially considered up to international standards of comfort. Hundreds more, aimed at budget travellers, may also be found along the seafront strip or a minute or two inland; these hotels usually lack some, but never all, of the extras like air-conditioning, private pools or playgrounds. But even in the luxury hotels the atmosphere is always casual.

You can spend the day snoozing under a thatched umbrella or a palm tree on the beach but it's hard to stay aloof from the activity aroun children riding horses, midget elephant, along sand; salesmen coming by offer sarongs, beads, hammocks, food and drink; itinerant masseuses who practise old-fashioned punching and stretching of tired tendons; Thai picnickers listening to exotic but catchy tunes.

With sea sports so fully developed along the main Pattaya beach, the shallow waterline gets crowded at times. Former fishing trawlers, spruced up a bit for the tourist trade, are beached in hopes of a charter. Swimmers and pedal-boat voyagers venture forth, keeping a careful watch for the sputtering sea-scooters. Windsurfers maintain a precarious balance in the waves created by speedboats and water-skiers.

The dividing line between sea sports and land sports is blurred by the popularity of parasailing—a sea-and-air sport which starts and ends on the beach. A fast motorboat propels the brave flyer, attached to a red-and-white parachute on the end of a long cable, high above the bay. The landing, which must avoid power lines and coconut palms, is said to be the delicate part.

Another recently developed sport is deep-sea fishing. It had

...ccurred to the Pattaya ...en that anyone would ... to fish for fun. Amateurs ...w bring back sizable marlin ...nd delicious snapper. Other boats take excursionists to nearby islands for swimming and snorkelling in superb, clear seas. The largest island, **Ko Larn,** is 45 minutes from Pattaya by converted trawler, twice as fast by speedboat. You can explore the underwater world in a glass-bottomed boat, gazing at vivid tropical fish and

coral, now depleted by invisible pollution. Scuba expeditions may begin here for a workout but generally go farther afield for excitement.

Organized excursions ashore take in the countryside to the east, heading toward the Cambodian border, with visits to rubber plantations and a large mining operation for precious stones. Another tour goes to an elephant kraal where a round-up is simulated and the well-trained beasts show off their skills.

Shopping is conveniently centred on the main street of south Pattaya and in fashionable boutiques attached to the luxury hotels. Off-the-peg and quickly tailored fashions, coral and shells, jewellery and trinkets catch the eye. A local product considered to be very chic is a pair of Thai fisherman's trousers, perhaps the world's floppiest, for men or women in fashion's vanguard.

Pattaya's restaurants serve superlative seafood—oysters, clams, shrimp, prawns, crabs, lobster and many types of meaty fish. At luxury hotels the

Straw hat—or parasol—is sensible under hot sun on beach in Pattaya. Note parasailing chute in the sky.

setting and preparation are likely to enhance the raw material; at simple waterfront restaurants the seafood's the same but the prices are also delightful. Tourists desperate for bratwurst, cannelloni or French fries find satisfaction up and down the strip. But some of the tastiest and cheapest food anywhere is served at the noodle stalls along the beach.

Nightlife, too, has something for every taste—big musical productions at the hotel nightclubs or soft music in intimate bars. One aspect of Pattaya's fame remains the abundance of pretty Thai girls cheerfully available and eager

to please. The action is concentrated in south Pattaya, which swings until 1 a.m.

Hua Hin

Across the Gulf of Siam from Pattaya, the resort of **Hua Hin** has long been a favourite of the royal family as well as ordinary Thais. In recent times it has taken on some glitter of international sophistication. The long white beach is still the prime attraction, but foreigners are also drawn to the fascinations of the town itself and the fishing port. The diversions at Hua Hin range from golf to pony rides.

North-East of Bangkok

A three- to four-hour drive from Bangkok's heat and tumult is the cool, calm resort of **Khao Yai.** This national park covering some 800 square miles shelters more than 100 species of wildlife protected by Thai law. Conservation is taken seriously: arriving tourists' cars are inspected for firearms. At Khao Yai (meaning Big Mountain) the hunting is strictly with cameras. Safaris are organized at night with bright searchlights to pick out deer, rare tropical birds and—with a lot of luck—free-roaming tigers, bears or elephants.

Khao Yai, 205 kilometres north-east of Bangkok, was proclaimed a national park in 1959. Before that it was notorious as a sanctuary for outlaws as well as animals. An 18-hole golf course, a restaurant and relatively sophisticated living quarters have been added to the natural appeal of the lush plateau. (Reservations for the motor lodge may be made at the head office of the Tourism Authority of Thailand,

Not terrorists nor phantoms, but street-sweepers fighting the dust.

Ratchadamnoen Nok Avenue, Bangkok.)

Though its official, hard-to-pronounce name is Nakhon Ratchasima, you'll be understood if you refer to this agreeable but unexciting town as KORAT. About 260 kilometres north-east of Bangkok, it's the base for an important archaeological excursion. Otherwise, only two items in the town are notable:

In the main square, on a high pedestal, stands a statue of Khunying Mo, a heroine of the early 19th century. Captured by invaders from Laos, she led the local women in a plot which subdued the enemy.

On the outskirts of Korat is a controversial modern Buddhist temple, **Wat Sala Loi.** Though clearly Thai, the design calls to mind contemporary Western church architecture. Inside is a great white Buddha as big as a house.

The ruins of the ancient religious compound of **Phimai** sprawl in the sun, blackened as if by fire—but perhaps by time alone. The site is at the end of the long, dusty main street of Phimai, some 60 kilometres north-east of Korat.

The main **shrine,** in the centre of the walled complex, was most likely designed by Khmer architects of the 11th or

Pedicabs replace taxis in Phimai, site of ancient Khmer-style shrine.

12th century. The style of the brick and stone buildings resembles that of the Angkor complex across the border in Kampuchea (formerly Cambodia). The fascinating **statu-** ary both in and outside of the central sanctuary indicates it was a sacred place for both Hindus and Buddhists. In other parts of the compound you'll find unrestored and puzzling fragments: big bullet-shaped stones strewn here and there, and long rows of stark, square windows.

A pleasant postscript (about 1 km. east of Phimai) is a **banyan tree** bigger than a circus tent. In its shade you can be served a meal or a drink—but only in the dry season. During the rainy season the nearby reservoir inundates the picnic ground. If spirits live in trees, as many Thais believe, then this prodigious banyan must be thronged with ghosts. The nearby chapel enjoys great renown.

Central Thailand

You might expect to find a statue or ceremonial fountain right in the centre of town, but in **Lop Buri** (154 km. north of Bangkok) you come upon a miniature Angkor Wat. The **Prang Sam Yod** (Temple of Three Towers) is a reasonably well-preserved example of ancient Khmer architecture. It first served as a Hindu shrine, then became a Buddhist sanctuary.

One of the old capitals of the Khmer people, Lop Buri flourished under Thai rule in the 17th century. King Narai chose the town as his alternate capital in case something happened to Ayutthaya. His caution proved fully warranted when Ayutthaya fell to the Burmese a century later. With the help of

Within walking distance, on the bank of the Moon River is an **archaeological garden** with a bumper crop of ancient statues, friezes, lintels and stone carvings of Buddha, gods, elephants, lions, monkeys and warriors. The exhibits in this open-air museum come from all over north-east Thailand.

French architects, Narai built a majestic palace complex known as **Phra Narai Rajanivet.** It is protected by high walls with imposing gateways. The distinctive niches in the walls are for candles during periods of festival. The palace compound has inner walls, on which local and tourist children romp, and the remains of gateways, houses and a reservoir. Two buildings now compose a **museum** containing, among other items, statues of old Lop Buri. The size of the palace precinct indicates the importance and prosperity of the 17th-century capital. Documents from the era show that foreign visitors including the ambassador of Louis XIV were greatly impressed by this place they called Louvo.

Back in the centre of town, opposite the city gate, the modern chapel of San Phra Kan stands on the site of an ancient shrine. For years the local faithful have been leaving offerings, especially food, for the Hindu deity within. A large troop of friendly monkeys has been taking advantage of this free lunch facility. If you buy a bunch of bananas (for sale at the temple)

In Lop Buri chapel, monkey steals garland offered to a Hindu deity.

you'll make a hundred little friends. But mind they don't steal your fruit—or your handbag.

The modern town of Sukhothai (about 450 km. north of Bangkok) is a very ordinary provincial market town of about 15,000 people. But 13 kilometres to the west stands the original **Sukhothai,** the first capital of Thailand, now a city-sized archaeological park celebrating a good and happy age. Sukhothai, which means "dawn of happiness", thrived during the reign of the enlightened King Ramkamhaeng the Great in the late 13th and early 14th centuries. The king, a legendary warrior, diplomat, law-giver and patron of the arts, ruled a powerful, prosperous country from his elegant palace in Sukhothai.

By the 15th century the centre of political and economic might had shifted south to Ayutthaya, and by the 16th century Sukhothai was a ghost town. About 30 years ago the ancient capital was still covered with jungle, the outlines of the classical towers camouflaged by a heavy green overgrowth. Complete restoration of the vast historical park will take another decade.

Three-ply ramparts with moats surround the old city. **59**

Calling All Gourmets

Along the highway between ancient and modern Sukhothai the farm houses are equipped with what seem to be the tallest, most complicated TV antennas. But appearances are deceiving—and not just to humans. The towers, armed with bright fluorescent lights and nets, are traps for flying insects. The large water bugs which inhabit local rice fields are lured into the nets during the nights of the rainy season. They provide the basic ingredient for an aromatic and expensive sauce which is a favourite of Thai gourmets. The bugs are so highly valued that the locals can earn more as trappers than as farmers. Which explains the bright lights of Sukhothai.

Until very recently the defences were thought to be earthen, but a core of brick and stone has now been discovered.

An efficient starting place for a tour of Sukhothai is the **Ramkamhaeng National Museum** near the centre of the walled area. On show are stone and bronze Buddha sculptures from Sukhothai's prime, a collection of weapons, some examples of the ceramics the capital exported, and a section of its ancient pipeline system. You have to cross a moat to reach the ruins of the **Royal Palace** and of **Wat Mahathat,** the biggest and finest temple of Sukhothai. The main *chedi* tapers gracefully to its pinnacle, high above the tops of dozens of cylindrical stone columns standing around like defunct smokestacks.

South-east of Wat Mahathat a three-topped temple, **Wat Sri Sawai,** stays aloof behind a wall and across the moat. It is thought to have been built before the era of Ramkamhaeng, when the Khmers held sway in this area.

Wat Sri Chum is an open-air temple with a gigantic seated Buddha; each finger of the statue is as tall as a man. The walls of the sanctuary, 10 feet thick, contain a secret passage—off to the left just inside the entrance. It was used by the king, though for exactly what purpose is not clear.

If you've just come from the flatlands around Bangkok you'll welcome the novelty of **Wat Saphan Hin,** a shrine on a hill-with-a-view... and even a breeze. Saphan means bridge and Hin means stone. It's a long haul up the primitive stone steps leading to the summit on which stands a Buddha statue more than 40 feet tall.

Perhaps the moodiest part of Sukhothai is **Wat Chetupon,**

south of the main complex. Resident archaeologists sometimes drive out to these early 15th-century ruins at sunset, when the air begins to cool and all is silent except for a distant cowbell and the chatter of birds. However, officials warn foreign tourists not to visit any of the outlying monuments without notifying the local police station (opposite the National Museum). Robbers lurk around the isolated sites.

An important but lesser-known archaeological centre 55 kilometres north of Sukhothai, **Si Satchanalai** also dates from the age of Ramkamhaeng the Great. You have to cross the Yom River in a small ferryboat to reach the ancient walled town. The shrines here were decorated with beauty and originality, much of the elegant detail is still visible.

All around the area are ancient kilns in which a distinctive porcelain was fired centuries ago. The first Thai ceramics were produced in Sukhothai; Ramkamhaeng even invited Chinese technical advisers. But the clay was better around Si Satchanalai, and here the industry thrived.

With an airport and a first-class hotel, **Phitsanulok** (nearly 500 km. north of Bangkok) is a base for excursions to Sukho-thai and Si Satchanalai. Though it has a long history, Phitsanulok was all but wiped out in modern times. A new business district, built after the devastating fire, has no special charm, but the town's location astride the wide Nan River compensates. In the dry season the steeply sloping river banks are used to grow vegetables; in the rainy season the rich soil is all under water.

The great fire miraculously spared Phitsanulok's greatest monument, **Wat Mahathat.** For centuries, believers have been coming here to pray before the famous seated Buddha image of polished bronze, reputed to have great powers. Today the shrine is the scene of great animation as Thai tourists swarm into the sanctuary. To meet this demand, a variety of shops within the complex sell pendants, relics and other souvenirs of the venerated 14th-century statue. This business-like touch seems not to distract the crowds of believers from their devotions. Also in the grounds of the temple, a squad of Thai dancers in classical costume perform on commission from those whose prayers have been answered. Vendors of flowers, incense and snacks further enliven the atmosphere.

The North

Thailand's second-largest city, **Chiang Mai,** is pleasantly short on hustle and bustle. It has lush vegetation, stately houses and cheerful, fun-loving people. Everything is authentic, including the hill tribesmen you see waiting for buses in their colourful costumes.

Between October and late January visitors enjoy a bonus of perfect spring-like weather. (Nights which suggest sweaters are a tremendous novelty for tourists from sweltering Bangkok.) Chiang Mai's plateau, surrounded by Thailand's highest mountains, grows an abundance of fruits, vegetables and flowers of both temperate and tropical varieties. This northern area also produces the nation's prettiest girls. Some claim that the town of Lamphun has the most beauties per capita, others say San Kamphaeng, but there's no doubt that the ancient walled city of Chiang Mai is the centre of it all. In a kingdom renowned for its beauties, this is a dazzling distinction.

From Bangkok, Thai Airways jets to Chiang Mai in less than 2 hours. Air-conditioned express buses make the run in about 9 hours, the overnight express train in 14 hours.

King Mengrai the Great founded Chiang Mai, meaning new town, towards the end of the 13th century. According to one legend the city wall—parts of which can still be seen—was constructed by 90,000 men working round-the-clock in shifts. Mengrai also built many temples and fine buildings. Under his rule arts and crafts played an important part in the life of the northern towns, and they still do. Which is why shopping here is full of revelations and pleasures.

Like all Thai towns, Chiang Mai has its share of historic monasteries. Among the many *wats* worth a look, start off with three within the ancient square moat protecting the heart of the city:

King Mengrai himself founded **Wat Chiang Man** in the 13th century. It contains two well-known religious statues which were already ancient when this monastery was built. A railing, bars and glass protect the precious images known as the Crystal Buddha and the Marble Buddha. At the rear of this temple is a *chedi* surrounded by sculptured elephants.

The huge *chedi* of **Wat Chedi Luang** bears witness to a disaster which struck Chiang Mai more than 400 years ago. The top of the pagoda came tumbling down, it seems, in a great earthquake. It was never restored, but, even so, what remains is still a very tall landmark.

In **Wat Prasingh,** a small chapel contains a treasured Buddha image, one of three ancient statues in existence called Phra Buddha Singh. The monastery's 14th-century library is decorated with admirable carving and sculpture.

But the most famous temple, **Wat Phrathat,** is at the end of an exciting zigzag mountain road... a 25-minute bus ride up from Chiang Mai. Until pious volunteers built the road in

1934 it was a very long walk from town. It's still some 300 steps from the parking area to the monastery itself, which stands about 3,400 feet above sea-level. Over the centuries pilgrims have been coming to the central gold *chedi*, marked by royal bronze parasols at each corner, to pay homage to the Buddha relics locked within. The cloister is lined with many Buddha statues of artistic importance. Aside from the historical, religious and aesthetic values of Doi Suthep, it offers a glorious **view** over the hills and valleys and Chiang Mai.

On a hilltop beyond Doi Suthep is the **Winter Palace,** where the Thai king spends several months of the year. When the royal family is away, the grounds are open to the public on weekends and holidays. The admirable gardens offer a lavish layout of flowers from many climes.

Travel agencies in Chiang Mai run excursions to another popular tourist attraction in the same area—a hamlet occupied by members of the Meo tribe. This is the most easily accessible of all the **hill tribe villages** in Thailand, so foreign influences have left their mark. For instance, the villagers now demand payment for posing for photos. Otherwise, they are friendly and apparently pleased that their colourful bejewelled costumes and simple huts are a centre of attention.

Saffron-robed monks in Chiang Mai gather before finely carved building in old monastery complex. **65**

In the centre of Lamphun a large, historic monastery called **Wat Prathat Haripoonchai** remains a busy educational and meditational establishment. The huge gold *chedi* in the middle of the monastery was begun more than a thousand years ago. The workmen who built it put together their own, simpler *chedi* outside the compound; trees now sprout from its ruins. A national **museum** nearby, in modern Thai architecture, has a collection of sculptures from the Lamphun district dating from the 10th to 12th centuries. One unusual exhibit: a Chinese slender-barrelled cannon of the Ming dynasty.

A pedicab will take you from the centre of Lamphun to **Wat Ku Kut.** This temple is said to have been founded by Princess Chamadevi, who ruled the Mon kingdom of Lamphun well over a thousand years ago. The most memorable of the original elements is a *chedi* rising in five tiers with a total of 60 standing Buddha images of stucco round the sides. Some of the statues have been restored to unnaturally perfect condition.

Lampang, nearly 100 kilometres south-east of Chiang Mai, is more restful than most provincial towns. In keeping with the easy pace, pony-drawn carriages compete with the motorized taxis. Lampang's history goes back a long way. It was a capital of the ancient Mon kingdom, before the Thai people arrived in the country. In the 16th century Lampang attained a mystic sort of renown because of a stubborn elephant. According to the story, the greatly revered statue called the Emerald Buddha was being transported to Chiang Mai when the elephant refused to go beyond Lampang. This was interpreted as a divine signal, so the image was installed in the town. Eventually the Emerald Buddha reached its present perch in Bangkok's Grand Palace.

Three Lampang temples deserve special mention. **Wat Phra Fang** has a tall white *chedi* with seven small shrines around the base. **Wat Phra Keo Don Tau,** which also shows Burmese influence, boasts excellent carvings. Out of town, **Wat Phra That Lampang Luang** enjoys a scenic riverside setting; aside from fine bronze and woodwork, the monastery's museum contains an emerald Buddha said to be made from the same piece of stone as the illustrious statue now in Bangkok.

Chiang Rai, Thailand's northernmost provincial capital, is easily reached from Chiang Mai, which lies some 180 kilometres away. You can travel by plane or bus but not by train, since the railway system doesn't venture that far. Or, for a dash of adventure, you can take a four- or five-hour bus ride from Chiang Mai to the end-of-the-world town of THA THON. There a sign in English asks tourists to register with the police, beware of pickpockets, concluding with the ultimate warning: "Don't moved far alone, will have danger from the murder may be".

At Tha Thon—barring a murder, of course—you can take a long-tailed boat for a ride on the Mae Kok River all the way down to Chiang Rai. Exciting rapids and the possibility of a raid by river bandits enliven the journey; sometimes the police provide an escort.

Chiang Rai looks something like an up-and-coming town in the American Midwest with its wide streets and new buildings; indeed the town plan was made by a missionary from the U.S. Though not the liveliest of places, it does have one nightclub, one prison and more tractor dealers than car dealers.

The far-sighted 13th-century King Mengrai the Great founded Chiang Rai, reportedly by chance. According to legend, his elephant ran loose and led him to a spot on the Mae Kok River; the scenery and military potential of the place inspired him to build a town. A statue of Mengrai stands at the east end of Chiang Rai. Like other Thai towns, Chiang Rai's history and treasure lies in its Buddhist temples. Several are set on hilltops with pleasant vistas of the town and river.

But Chiang Rai's own sights—including a vast covered market where you can buy fish dead or alive—are secondary to the regional attractions for which it is the base.

In the mountains north of Chiang Rai live villagers with one foot in the Iron Age, the other tentatively dipping into the age of the transistor. To see the really isolated hill tribes you have to be prepared to hike for hours or even days. But one **Akha village** on a hilltop near MAE CHAN is only 7 kilometres off the main highway along a very bumpy but passable (in the dry season) track.

Modern civilization has made few inroads here. Pigs, water buffalo and xenophobic dogs burrow among the stilt houses; women mill the rice by the same method used in the Stone Age; dozens of naked **69**

children, the offspring of the society's uninhibited marriageless relations, shyly ask the tourists for coins. The women, wearing regal beaded headdresses, try to sell the visitors jewellery, mostly made from melted-down coins. A sign in Thai at the entrance to the **70** hamlet prohibits photographing any opium smokers. The Akhas and other hill tribes lack enthusiasm for the Thai government's persistent campaigns to eliminate both the production and consumption of opium, the most lucrative crop in the hidden valleys of the north.

Between two villages is an

airy school where the students in their clean blue-and-white uniforms might be mistaken for any other Thai pupils. These are Akhas and Yaos being introduced to the mainstream of national life. But in spite of the government's efforts, few village children are sent to school.

The **Yao village,** of adobe

Painting an umbrella in Bor Sang; plough team near Golden Triangle.

huts with thatched roofs, seems no more sophisticated than the Meo or Akha hamlets. But a Yao elder turns out to be able to speak several tribal languages as well as Thai, and to read and **71** write Chinese. The women, wearing blue turbans and red collars on their jackets, rally en masse for any group of visitors—even for one person—to show their handicrafts. Dogs, pigs and children in bottomless costumes wander in and out of the scene.

Travel agencies in Chiang Rai run excursions to various hill villages, or you can make your own arrangements through your hotel or a taxi driver. You won't need any explanation of the wooden fertility statues, which would shock and demoralize any visiting missionary, but you might want to be told the significance of the big swing or the courting ground. A guide who can speak English and, if possible, the tribal tongue as well, can add greatly to the success of the trip. As for the villagers, they are friendly at best and at worst merely diffident.

The border town of **Chiang Saen,** staring across the Mekong River at Laos, has an unexpectedly pompous history. Between the 10th and 13th centuries it was the capital of a prosperous principality. Traces of the glorious past are scattered through what is now an undistinguished market town: the moated city wall, remains of temples in restoration or ruin, and a museum showing Stone Age implements and statues from the golden age of Chiang Saen.

Twelve kilometres beyond Chiang Saen you reach the evocatively named **Golden Triangle.** This is the three-way border of Thailand, Laos and Burma. There is no barbed wire, for the countries don't touch; the Mekong and its tributary, the Mae Sai, form the liquid frontiers. There is no legal crossing point at the Golden Triangle. Moreover, this region is infamous for the illegal crossings through which a torrential flow of opium passes on its way to the heroin traders of Paris and New York. In northern Thailand alone an estimated 25,000 acres of farmland are devoted to the cultivation of poppies. Actually, this is much less than it used to be, before government efforts to encourage diversification to less sinister crops. You won't see poppies growing here, for discretion confines the cultivation to less easily reached valleys. But the farms between Chiang Saen and the Golden Triangle legally produce another drug: tobacco.

Mae Sai is as far north as you can go in Thailand. If you find frontier posts dramatic, you'll want to see the international bridge, which carries mostly pedestrian traffic to and from Burma. The border is open to authorized travellers from 6 a.m. to 6 p.m. Tourists are only allowed as far as the halfway point on the bridge. All along the Thai side of the span, Burmese women sell the products they have "imported" by hand: oranges, packaged prunes, cheroots, lacquer boxes, ivory carvings and contraband cigarettes. A short walk south, in the centre of Mae Sai, a factory transforms chunks of Burmese jade into finely polished jewellery. Experts covet the jade of Burma, calling it the world's best.

The South

Southern Thailand, stretching narrowly down to Malaysia, gives you a choice of seas. The much longer eastern coast faces the familiar Gulf of Thailand, while the west is washed by the Indian Ocean. Either way you turn, you'll discover sensational beaches. And the land between—rice fields, coconut and rubber plantations—is as scenic as it is productive.

Architects of sand-castles on the beach at Phuket take inspiration from classic prangs *and* stupas.

THE SOUTH

CHUMPHON, BANGKOK

N

La-un

RANONG
ระนอง

Kra Buri

Kapoe
Tha Chana

Takua Pa

Chaiya

Kapong
Phanom

PHANGNGA
พังงา

Thap Put

SURAT THANI

Thalang
Ao Luk
Phrasaeng สุราษฎร์ธานี

PHUKET ภูเก็ต
Sichon

Laem
Prothep
Ban Song

Tha Sala

KRABI

Chawang

NAKHON
SI
THAMMARAT
นครศรีธรรมราช

Khlong Thom
Thung Song

Sikao
Huai Yot
Chian Yai

Kantang
TRANG
ตรัง
Hua Sai

Palian
PHATTHALUNG

Thung Wa

Langu
Kuan Kalong

SONGKHLA
สงขลา

Hat Yai
หาดใหญ่

SATUN
Chana

Sadao
PATTANI
ปัตตานี

Saba Yoi
Panare

ALOR STAR
Yaha

YALA
ยะลา

PENANG
Bannang

NARATHIWAT

BUTTERWORTH
Betong

Sungai Padi

Waeng

M A L A Y S I A

0   60   120 km

0   30   60   90 miles

Gulf of Thailand

A N D A M A N   S E A

Phuket

This lush hideaway island is in the process of joining the first rank of classic international resorts. In fact, some people think Phuket is becoming *too* popular. Hotels are under construction all over the place, as an invasion of tourists packs out the island's perfect beaches. The islanders, who stay in the shade and seldom learn to swim, are amused that people would fly thousands of miles just to baste and roast themselves and fill up on ordinary things like lobster and shrimps.

Phuket, pronounced poo-KET, is not totally insular: a causeway links it to the mainland of southern Thailand. This brings tourist coaches direct from Bangkok in about 15 hours. But the easy way to get here is by air. The trip from Bangkok to Phuket town takes a mere hour and a bit.

The highway south from the airport passes through a dusty village, THALANG, the site of the island's ancient capital. Burmese invaders besieged, pillaged and destroyed the original Thalang in 1809. In an earlier, more positive chapter of Thai history, the city withstood a Burmese siege which lasted more than a month. That battle, in 1786, made heroines of Lady Muk and her sister, Lady Chan. They commanded the defence of Phuket after Lady Muk's husband, the governor, died. Statues of the short-haired women warriors, garlanded with full honours, stand in a traffic circle down the road.

The new capital of the island, also called PHUKET or Phuket Town, is mostly utilitarian. Only one old street of traditional Sino-Portuguese two-storey houses has been preserved. It's named Thalang Road.

Thailand's biggest island, a province all by itself, Phuket is 47 miles long and 15 miles at its widest. The population, well above 100,000, is a cosmopolitan mix of Thais, Chinese, Malaysians, Indians, mysterious "Sea Gypsies" who keep to themselves and a few Europeans. The island's 500-year-old tin-mining industry remains a big operation by land and by sea. The economy also relies on coconut and rubber production: much of the island is covered by graceful palms or military formations of rubber trees covering the ground with cool, dark shadows.

But the reason tourists travel all the distance from Bangkok to Phuket is the clear sea. The best beaches are on the west coast of the island, where fine white sand slopes very gradually into the Indian Ocean's Andaman Sea. The only relatively built-up beach—hotels, bungalows, restaurants, some pubs and discos—is **Patong,** 15 kilometres west of Phuket Town by paved road. The marvellous beaches of **Kamala, Karon, Kata** and **Nai Harn** are less developed, and, until the island's road network is upgraded, they are destined to stay slightly remote at the end of dirt tracks. This is just fine with vacationers who appreciate some elbow room at the expense of a bumpy ride.

Thirty or so uninhabited islands enliven the sea views from Phuket—no boring, bare horizons here. At several beaches proprietors of long-tailed boats offer excursions for picnics or snorkelling. Local scuba experts qualify the undersea scene as first-rate, with plenty of coral and brilliantly hued fish. Deep-sea fishing expeditions can be organized; droves of sailfish, barracuda and mackerel are hooked.

Local souvenir shops also stress the wonders of the sea. They sell coral, remarkable sea-shells and locally cultivated pearls—and counterfeit pearls, too.

Nobody has ever chosen Phuket for the nightlife. But the major hotels have regular entertainment—and indoor and outdoor dining can also be festive. The fresh seafood is memorable, working up to Phuket lobster, much appreciated and highly priced in far-off Bangkok. For dessert, don't pass up the local pineapple—small, sweet and so tender that the core is eaten.

The perfect start to any evening's program is the tropical sunset. The most dramatic vantage point—even islanders sometimes turn up to watch—is a promontory called **Laem Promthep,** 19 kilometres southwest of Phuket Town. Photo fans will find a single majestic palm standing ready to frame the sunset. A fishing boat or two will probably putter into the picture just as the last red smudge fades. Even if you call it an early night under the brilliant stars, you've already seen the best show in town.

Excursions

Travel agencies in Phuket mount several different day-long excursions. Two of the tours are exceptionally interesting:

Phangnga, the province just north of Phuket, has some of the most exotic scenery in all Thailand, much of it at sea. Long-tailed boats skim through the mangrove into a dreamscape of mad mountain-tops poking from the bay. At two points of the journey the boats

In the south: fantastic scenery (Phangnga Bay) and sunny faces.

sail through tunnels the tides have worn beneath limestone islands, Then in a natural indentation in the sheer side of the island called KHAO KHIAN, you can see a man-made curiosity: paintings similar to the prehistoric cave frescoes of Europe. The origin is unknown.

The tours can only highlight a few of the 100 fantastic

77

islands and islets in the bay. Almost all are uninhabited, though souvenir stands materialize on the beach at KHAO PHINGKAN.

The excursion boats stop for lunch at a thoroughly implausible place, the island of **Panyi.** Here Moslem fishing people have established a village on stilts above the sea; the only habitable area on the "mainland" of the rocky island is used as a cemetery and grazing ground for goats. Tourists are welcome to roam the wooden walkways serving as streets, looking in on the simple houses, a school, the shrimp-drying activities and the shops. Visitors from as far away as Bangkok and Singapore rush to buy the island's smelly shrimp paste. Lunch at one of the tourist-oriented stilt restaurants consists of seafood, normally of excellent quality.

A separate excursion goes to the much more southerly island called **Ko Phi Phi** (sometimes advertised as P. P. Island). Sea cliffs high above the waves are home for a big population of sea swallows. Others live in a vast cave inside a neighbouring island. The nests which the birds keep building so industriously at great altitudes are collected by the islanders at considerable risk to human life. It's

a profitable export business, supplying far-flung Chinese restaurants with the raw material for that great and expensive delicacy, birds' nest soup.

Otherwise, there's not much to do on Ko Phi Phi but relax on the beautiful beach or take a snorkel tour of the wonders of the coral reef.

Hat Yai

The Malaysian border is only 50 kilometres south of Hat Yai, a booming, swinging frontier town of about 100,000 population. Tourists from Malaysia and Singapore crowd the shops for big savings on Thai food, clothing and household appliances. Visitors from Bangkok stock up on bargains from across the border, priced to suggest that a certain amount of smuggling goes on. Hat Yai (sometimes spelled Haadyai) is also proud of its intensive, uninhibited and economically priced nightlife.

An exotic daytime attraction may be seen on the first or second Sunday of any month: **bullfighting,** Thai style. This southern speciality has nothing to do with the Spanish national fiesta. It's a battle of wits and bull-headed will-power between two fighting bulls. They lock horns and struggle interminably for superiority. A shifting hind leg, a pulsating muscle, a twisting horn—the slightest indication of a change in the situation animates the audience. Gamblers, making up the vast majority of the crowd, explode into urgently shouted readjustments of the odds. The bulls, trained to battle, react to the cheers of the crowd by trying even harder. Eventually one of the combatants sends a silent signal of surrender and backs away. Instead of pursuing him, the winner watches haughtily as his victim retreats. Visitors with no financial interest in the proceedings may find eight hours of bullfighting a bit much, but one or two matches are worth watching.

Hat Yai has a reclining Buddha of gargantuan proportions, a favourite goal of pilgrimages. The modern concrete statue is hollow, and you can enter the back and see that a huge heart and lungs have been sculpted within. A revered relic is encased in the heart. In the basement below the statue, religious souvenirs are sold.

Songkhla

Only 30 kilometres north-east of the excitements of Hat Yai, the port resort of Songkhla is a place for relaxing under the tropical moon. Mile after mile of unbroken white sand beach is surprisingly under-exploited. Songkhla's international renown comes nowhere near Phuket's—much less Pattaya's. This may be because the good swimming season is brief and occurs in the less fashionable months of March, April and May. In the windy season (August to January or February) this sector of the Gulf of Thailand is choppy. So everyone goes round the corner of the coast beyond the statue of a mermaid at **Samila Beach.** There the sands are protected, and the waterfront groves of pine and casuarina trees give shade to picnic grounds and outdoor seafood restaurants, formal gardens and a rather casual park with grazing cows.

On the far side of the peninsula, where Thailand's biggest lake meets the sea, the port of Songkhla is as colourful as its fleet of trawlers painted red, blue or green. You can watch them landing the giant prawns, and follow the iced seafood to market and to table.

Songkhla's **lake**—50 miles long and up to 16 miles wide—is worth exploring. Finding a suitable boat, though, takes some inquiries, for excursions follow no regular schedule. The tourist ship *Sakarina Nava*, in effect a floating seafood res- **79** taurant with room for about 40 gourmet-sightseers, can be chartered by the half-day or full day.

Any tour of the lake ought to take a break on **Ko Yo,** an island of flaming shrubs, trees heavy with fruit, and a scattered population of about 5,000. Mainlanders stock up on the local rambutan, durian and other delicious but forbidding-looking fruits. You can also wander into houses in which weaving is a cottage industry; the distinctive Ko Yo cloth may be bought on the spot—in spite of the non-commercial atmosphere.

Back in Songkhla, photo fans may feel obliged to visit a Moslem fishing village about 5 kilometres down the coast from Samila beach. There you'll find adorable dark-skinned girls and boys in sarongs and care-

Tourism has scarcely touched the sands and inland sea of Songkhla.

fully decorated fishing boats. Pictures can only hint at the village's other main distinction—thousands of fish drying in the sun along the dusty main street, creating an aroma that would bring an army to its knees.

Finally, two cultural attractions in Songkhla. The **Songkhla National Museum,** stocked with archaeological specimens from southern Thailand, occupies a nicely restored Chinese-style mansion. This century-old house alongside the ancient city wall served as the residence of governors and officials and was the regional administrative headquarters.

Another, more heteroclite museum has been established in the 400-year-old **Majimawat Monastery.** A Buddhist abbot with catholic tastes in art has collected an off-beat clutter of exhibits: Buddha statues, ancient pottery, stuffed snakes, and old rifles, swords, coins and skulls.

What to Do

Folklore

Thai folklore can be as incomprehensible as an atonal opera sung to the accompaniment of xylophones, oboes and gongs. Or as self-explanatory as no-holds-barred boxing.

You might stumble upon it anywhere: kite fighting in the centre of Bangkok; dancers in full regalia at a local shrine; or a company of roving players performing an obscure melodrama before the most unsophisticated small-town audience.

But first you ought to see one of the **folklore shows** staged expressly for tourists, in which the highlights are condensed and explained. These spectacles are often accompanied by a banquet of Thai food, also explained, adding up to twice the

---

Festivals

So many big and small, pompous or amusing festivals take place in Thailand that they could fill a book. Here's a brief sampling of events:

February to April. Kite fights above the Pramane Ground in Bangkok, every weekday afternoon.

February. Flower carnival in Chiang Mai: floats and parades.

April. Songkran (Water) Festival. Most uninhibitedly celebrated in Chiang Mai but also fun in suburban Bangkok.

May. Royal Ploughing Ceremony. The date, fixed by the king's Brahmin astrologers, comes just before the rainy season. The king presides over ceremonies and processions at Pramane Ground, Bangkok.

May. Boon Bong Fai (Rocket) festival. Drums, dances, fireworks. Mostly in the north-east.

July. Asanha Puja. Candlelit processions by full moon at every temple in Thailand.

October-November. Kathin, the end of the rainy season and Buddhist Lent. Processions carrying gifts of new robes and utensils to the monks.

November. Loi Krathong. During the full moon, candles and incense float on banana-leaf boats on rivers and canals everywhere, but especially Bangkok and Chiang Mai.

November. Elephant Round-up, Surin (north-east Thailand). Hundreds of elephants mobilized by the Tourism Authority of Thailand and provincial authorities.

The music may be inscrutable but the beautiful people and costumes make for an appealing spectacle.

pleasure and edification. The special performances usually feature the northern Thai "fingernail dance" in which golden fingernails double the length, and allure, of the women's eloquent fingers. And in classical or peasant costumes the same performers come back to execute war, sword, harvest and hill-tribe dances.

Thai **martial arts,** performed at these tourist shows, include battles with sharp sticks and sharper swords. A ritual always precedes the bout: the fighters kneel to pay homage to their instructors and to invoke the help of the spirits, all to the accompaniment of oboes and drums.

The unique sport of **Thai boxing** may be seen at folklore shows or at stadiums in Bangkok and other towns. Only kangaroos could outdo these kickers and punchers, who use their elbows, knees and feet in addition to gloved fists. Here, too, the pre-bout ritual is essential.

Thai boxing is the occasion for spirited betting. So are cockfighting and fish-fighting and, in the south, bullfighting (all outlawed within Bangkok's city limits). **85**

Sports

In Thailand's tropical swelter it would be madness to exert oneself under the midday sun. Still, Bangkok alone has nine **golf** courses. Best to go out at dawn.

Tennis courts are found at the big hotels. Some of them have lights.

Most of the year there is **horse-racing** at Bangkok's two royal racetracks. Saturdays and Sundays.

Betting also surrounds **Thai boxing,** viewable almost every evening in Bangkok and some provincial towns. Good seats are quite expensive; no charge for the music and ritual.

Many hotels have **swimming** pools. Bangkok's Siam Park pool offers swimming and recreation in a top tropical setting. At seaside resorts, in addition, hotels or nearby entrepreneurs can provide equipment for water sports old and new.

Fishing has only recently been exploited as a sport in Thailand, so you may not find specialized equipment for battling sailfish or sharks. But if all you want is a day lolling on the deck of a boat with a rod and reel for the mackerel, snapper or parrotfish, it can easily be arranged.

Parasailing, something like water-skiing in the sky, is a big success in Pattaya.

Sailboats with holiday-coloured sails can be rented at some beaches. So can other vehicles, such as pedal-boats and peppy little water scooters.

Scuba diving is practised and taught at the major resorts. If you have five days to devote to it you can rise from gross beginner to internationally certified undersea diver.

Water-ski fans will find equipment and powerful boats at popular beaches.

Windsurfing, combining a surfboard with a hand-held sail, requires great coordination, but instruction is offered (15 hours for a diploma).

Shopping

From amethysts to zircons, from antiques to stuffed toy zebras, shopping in Thailand is a kaleidoscope of temptations. The range of bargains prompts the official propaganda to dub Bangkok a shopper's paradise. Perhaps, but only when it comes to indigenous products. If it's duty-free sensations you're after—imported cameras, hi-fi and perfumes—you'd better schedule a stop in Hong Kong or Singapore.

Where to Shop
The Tourism Authority of Thailand issues a free booklet "Official Shopping Guide", full of advice, suggestions and lists of recommended shops. It divides Bangkok into seven shopping areas, which essentially surround the leading hotels. Indeed, each of the big hotels has its own shopping arcade for tourists lacking time or inclination to leave the air-conditioning. But the shops outside, though not necessarily any cheaper, add a touch of adventure to the exercise.

The tourist-oriented shops are only a starting point for the serious shopper. The big department stores have handicrafts and other possibilities at fixed prices—a relief to those **87** who hate bargaining, an indicator to those who want to go forth and haggle elsewhere.

Outdoor markets are fascinating even for the non-shopper. The biggest of all is the Weekend Market at Bangkok's Chatuchak Park on Phaholyothin Road (near the Northern Bus Terminal), open Saturdays and Sundays 7 a.m.–6 p.m. Bangkok's Thieves' Market—actually part of Chinatown—with its tiny shops and stalls full of necessities, luxuries and mysteries, is the place to find the antique dealers.

If you're planning to go "up-country"—outside of Bangkok—save some time for shopping. Prices tend to be lower on locally produced articles. In northern Thailand you can visit the workshops and see the handicrafts being made. At the sea resorts there are bargains in seashells and coral.

When to Shop

Everyday, including Sunday, shopping is a non-stop affair. In some neighbourhoods and resorts, the small shops stay open as late as 10 p.m. The weekend market keeps going from dawn on Saturday to Sunday night. Chinatown is liveliest Monday to Saturday. See the Hours section of the Blueprint for details.

Do's and Don'ts

No matter what a merchant tells you, or doesn't bother to tell you, please bear in mind that it is utterly forbidden to take a Buddha image out of Thailand... not just antiques but *any* Buddha image in any form.

Antiques and genuine works of art can't be exported without a special certificate (see p. 113).

Disregard touts who propose to help you with your shopping; they receive a commission from the shop owners, raising your price.

Bargaining is the rule almost everywhere (starting with the taxi that takes you shopping). If you consider posturing and negotiating a game, then bargaining can be amusing. Try to disguise your own feelings, especially when you truly crave something. Be relaxed and cheerful, never in a hurry, never anxious to close a deal. If the price is too high, never scowl; smile or laugh at the ridiculous suggestion. The shop owner is likely to smile or laugh as he concedes your point. In the game of bargaining, your patience and good humour are worth real money.

In Chiang Mai workshop, intricate touches are added to silver bowl.

What to Buy

Antiques. For the informed collector, worthwhile objects from Thailand, Burma, Cambodia, China and Laos may be found—at the Thieves' Market or in posh shops or in the provinces. Experts at the National Museum in Bangkok meet the public on Sundays and Mondays to vouch for the authenticity of works of art or antiquity. Export permission is required for genuine antiques or art treasures. See p. 113.

Art. Paintings in several media by Thai artists, usually on familiar rice paddy or temple spire themes, are sold at galleries and shops all over. Temple stone rubbings on rice paper are another topical souvenir.

Artificial flowers. No joke —Thailand not only grows some of the world's most beautiful living flowers, it also exports great quantities of hand-made imitations.

Bronze. A great Thai tra-

dition, now used for rust-free tableware as well as lamps, bells, candelabra and statues.

Ceramics. Special wood is used to fire the kilns which bake celadon, a distinctive Thai pottery. Porcelain figurines are also made here. Ming and Ching dynasty bowls and shards turn up, salvaged from the river at Ayutthaya and Sukhothai; so do imitations.

Dolls. Thai dancers in or out of formal costumes, peasant women in sampans, hill tribe costumes, animal figures.

Elephants. A favourite Thai symbol, the elephant is immortalized in wood carvings from thumb-sized to life-sized, in jade and in flashy models studded with glass.

Fashion. Custom tailoring—allegedly in 24 hours or less—can be a solid bargain in Thailand. But try to give the tailor several days or even a week if you want a really good garment. Dresses, suits, slacks, shirts, safari suits—even bikinis—can be made to measure. Women's ready-to-wear shops often sell good, cheap local copies of the latest European fashions. Men's tropical sports shirts in loud designs may also be bought off the peg.

Gems. Thailand mines precious stones (sapphires and rubies) while others are imported at favourable prices from Burma, India, Sri Lanka and similar sources. Bangkok claims to be the world's top gem-cutting centre. For any purchase of magnitude, seek out a reputable shop and avoid unlikely bargains.

Handicrafts. With skill, patience and ingenuity, Thai artisans produce a seemingly endless variety of hand-crafted objects. Each region has its specialities, from the embroidery of northern hill tribes to the silk weaving of the south.

Ivory. Chinese-style elephant sculptures, Mandarin figurines, as well as incredible one-piece globe-within-globe-within-globe follies.

Jewellery. Thai designers tend toward traditional tastes, but originals can be ordered. Choose carefully where you shop; establishments where tour buses stop often pay the travel agency a 30 per cent kickback. Thai costume jewellery, including imitation jewels, can be good and cheap.

Kites. Fierce fighting models, neatly folded for easy packing, make an original gift.

Lacquerware. Pretty little

At Bangkok's vast weekend market exotic flowers are everyday joys.

gold and black boxes in the shape of fantasy animals, or multi-coloured bowls and plates.

Mobiles. Cheerful, imaginative hanging ensembles such as stylized bamboo fishes; or bells of shell that tinkle in the breeze.

Niello ware. A black metal alloy inlaid on silver for trinkets or works of art.

Old books. Illuminated Burmese manuscripts on parchment, folded accordion-style in leather bindings.

Treadle-pumping Meo villager turns out brightly coloured handicrafts.

Pottery. A characteristic Thai variety, *benjarong* ware, has a five-coloured design on white, grey or black background. Also patterned porcelain jars, plates, pots, even spittoons.

Quilted jackets. Oriental style cotton wrap-arounds in bright colours.

Rattan goods. Lightweight furniture; peasant hats.

Seashells. Collectors can buy notable bargains at Thai beach resorts, in shops or from itinerant vendors.

Tape cassettes. Thai, international pop and classical music at bargain prices; presumably some dealers cut expenses by counterfeiting.

Thai silk. Happy silkworms keep thousands of nimble weavers busy, hand and foot, producing the famous, colourful Thai fabrics. From the most delicate blouses to heavy bedspreads, the long-lasting fibres live up to their worldwide reputation. Durable Thai cotton, mostly factory-made, goes into popular ready-to-wear clothes, tablecloths, towels and toys.

Umbrellas. Around Chiang Mai they make hand-painted parasols, big and small—to your own design if you wish.

Woodcarvings. Teak salad bowls, furniture, figurines and knick-knacks.

Xylophones. The Thai versions, called *ranad ek* and *ranad thum* (treble and alto respectively), have wooden bars on a boat-shaped soundbox.

Zoological curiosities. Mounted butterflies with Latin captions; stuffed cobras poised to strike; stuffed mongooses as antidote.

Nightlife

For a town that closes its bars at midnight (1 a.m. on weekends), Bangkok crams in plenty of nightlife. Enthusiasts fly in from halfway around the world to sample the excitement. They fly out tired but happy.

But first, a word about family entertainment. Nightclubs, primarily in the major hotels, feature live bands, floor shows and dancing. Bangkok also has discos as well as more intimate bars with combo or piano music, plus bars and pubs for friendly conversation.

Various nightclub-style restaurants specialize in traditional Thai food and music; the floor show consists of classical Thai dancing or regional folklore or both.

Otherwise, the cultural possibilities for foreign visitors are quite limited. Visiting musicians occasionally perform, as do local theatre groups. Because of a stiff tax on imported films, very few are shown. This is supposed to encourage the Thai film industry, which still pours forth hundreds of second-rate movies. Some bars, clubs, hotels and associations fill the gap by showing imported films on a semi-private basis. Check listings in the English-language newspapers.

The Go-Go Scene

Bangkok-by-Night, primarily a man's world, lives up to its reputation. The unabashed sensuality of the girlie bars is mellowed by an almost non-commercial conviviality. Judicious policing keeps clip joints from operating for long. The go-go dancers seem to like their work, they appear pleased to be offered a drink (not exorbitantly priced), and they cheerfully continue to be natural and friendly wherever developments lead. Though these bars are clearly designed to serve male customers, women are normally welcome to come in for a drink and a look. Some "gay" bars now operate in the same areas, especially around Patpong.

For better or worse, massage parlours have brought almost as much fame to Thailand as orchids and spired architecture. Though they are invariably listed under "nightlife" these establishments provide all-around services for sybarites from lunchtime to midnight closing. Setting the tone, parlours display the staff masseuses—sometimes clad in evening gowns!—behind one-way glass near the entrance.

The more elegant parlours advertise that women customers are also served. And Bangkok has conventional health clubs, too, for old-fashioned muscle-toning without the "extras" for which Thailand's masseuses are celebrated.

No summary of Bangkok nightlife would be complete without a paragraph on the dangers and annoyances, large and trivial. Pimps, including many taxi drivers, always have enticing suggestions; these are usually more expensive than what you had in mind. Touts who hang around outside hotels and bars know where to find live sex shows and other pornographic diversions. However, these are technically illegal and could be raided by the police. And beware of transvestites, often in cars, who prey on gullible tourists; among other things, they tend to rob their "clients".

Provincial nightlife is usually calmer than in Bangkok, though many towns have nightclubs with hostesses for hire, massage parlours and the like. Pattaya has a comprehensive nightlife comparing favourably with Bangkok's. Hat Yai, in the far south, outdoes all other provincial towns with a highly concentrated entertainment zone that attracts crowds of tourists from across the border in Malaysia—where sin is more expensive.

Dining

Thai food is wholesome, delicious and inexpensive. But it ought to be X-rated—too spicy for children or the weak-hearted. Still, you don't have to take the plunge at your first meal. Nobody will accuse you of cowardice if you remove the slices of tiny red and green peppers from your soup and sauce. Or you can begin with the tourist version of Thai cuisine, specially subdued for foreign palates, before you escalate to the fiery truth of the real thing.

You can vary your diet with fabulous fresh fruit and plain unaffected seafood—even lob-

ster is within reach of many a tourist budget. Homesick appetites can find the reassurance of hamburgers, pizzas or sukiyaki—at least in Bangkok and sophisticated resorts. And in the most provincial village you can usually find good Chinese food for a bit of bland relief from all the chillies.

As wide as the range of cuisines is the choice of atmosphere. You can learn about Thai flavours in lavish, authentic surroundings to the tune of traditional music. Or you can pick up a snack at a pushcart on which, amazingly, a cook is producing perfect paper-thin mini-pancakes over a charcoal brazier. Somewhere between these extremes are simple restaurants, often in open air, where the menu, if any, is written in Thai only. Point to what looks good and the momentum will take you from there. Noodle shops alone occupy six pages of the Bangkok telephone directory.

The prices on the menus in restaurants catering for the tourist trade are not quite what they seem. Usually a service charge and tax are added to the

Among pleasures of the outdoor life, food stalls and pushcarts put a snack-on-a-stick in easy reach.

bill, and an additional 10 per cent tip is appropriate. Ironically, the cheap, non-air-conditioned, non-tourist places don't add a service charge—and the waiters don't expect tips.

What to Eat
Take a tip from the Thais and eat plenty of steamed rice along with all the hot dishes. This helps to smother the fire of the chilli peppers. In fact there's no substitute, certainly not cold drinks.

But dwelling on the pungency of Thai food is unfair. There are admirable, subtle undertones. To complement the peppers, Thai chefs choose from an imaginative rainbow of flavourful basics: basil, coconut milk, coriander, cinnamon, garlic, lemon grass, lime juice, nutmeg and usually sugar. Almost all the surprises are delightful.

Appetizers. *Paw pia tod*[1] is a Thai spring roll, a delicate, crisp pancake encircling a sweet-and-sour delight of pork, crabmeat and bean sprouts.

Gai hor bai toey[2] consists of chunks of chicken fried with sesame oil, soya sauce, oyster sauce, herbs and perhaps a drop of whisky, served inside a leaf wrapper.

Soup. *Tom yam*[3], a hot-

97

sour soup made with either pork, shrimp, beef, chicken or fish, must be accompanied by plenty of steamed rice to soak up the excess chilli flavour. Notice the fanciful selection of herbs and leaves floating in the big bowl.

Gaeng jeud[4] is a less pungent soup of chicken, pork and shrimp cooked with Chinese-style vegetables plus Thai herbs and spices.

Rice and noodles. *Kao pad*[5] is fried rice with whatever chunks of meat come to hand.

Mee grob[6] means crispy-fried rice noodles with shrimp, pork, bean sprouts, egg, and a sweet-and-sour taste.

Bah mee nam[7] is a rich broth containing thin noodles, pork or chicken chunks, bean sprouts, herbs and restrained spices. A filling soup that's more like a main dish.

Seafood. *Hor mok pla*[8], a fish curry with vegetables and coconut milk, served wrapped in banana leaves.

Pla preow wan[9] is fresh fish,

fried and covered in a thick sweet-and-sour sauce.

Gung tod[10], crispy fried prawns, usually comes with a choice of sauces.

Meat. *Gaeng mud-sa-man*[11], a beef curry that's less spicy than most and has an overtone of peanuts.

Kao nah gai[12] is a sliced chicken dish with spring onion and bamboo shoots atop steamed rice.

Sa lad neua san[13] translates as roast beef salad but aside from cold beef and vegetables you'll find chillies, garlic and perhaps mint.

Sweets. *Salim*[14]. Coconut milk and crushed ice refresh this dish of sugared noodles.

Ice-cream, pronounced ice-cream[15], sometimes comes in original natural flavours; a local variation of a sundae would be coconut ice-cream sprinkled with peanuts and kernels of maize.

Fruits. *Som-o*[16], translated pomelo, is a tropical cousin of a grapefruit, served sectioned.

---

1. ปอเปี๊ยะทอด   2. ไก่ห่อใบเตย   3. ต้มยำ   4. แกงจืด

5. ข้าวผัด   6. หมี่กรอบ   7. บะหมี่น้ำ   8. ห่อหมกปลา

9. ปลาเปรี้ยวหวาน   10. กุ้งทอด   11. แกงมัสมั่น   12. ข้าวหน้าไก่

13. สลัดเนื้อสัน   14. สลิ่ม   15. ไอสครีม   16. ส้มโอ

98 17. สับปะรด

Sup-pa-rod[17], pineapple, is an old familiar fruit but twice as lively on its home ground.

The more exotic indigenous fruits are rarely found in restaurants but may be discovered at markets and street stalls. You don't have to know the correct name, just point:

Ngor (rambutan) looks like a nightmarishly overdeveloped hairy strawberry; the fruit is hidden inside.

Lamut, a light-brown fruit that needs peeling, is syrupy sweet, reminiscent of the taste of fresh fig.

Durian, a monster with spiky thorns, contains bits of custard-like fruit around egg-shaped pits; the odour is widely considered more oppressive than any old cheese.

And look for delicious local oranges, bananas, papayas, mangoes... almost any fruit you can imagine except northerly apples and pears, which are imported and expensive.

Curiosities

Thai restaurants often welcome their customers with cold, sometimes frozen, hand-towels as a relief from the tropical world outside. In recent times many restaurants have taken to issuing disposable mini-towels in small plastic packets. The explosions you hear all about you are caused by Thais smacking the air-tight packs to open them.

Salt-shakers are rarely found on Thai dinner tables. If you find the food under-salted, add some of the caramel-coloured fish sauce, *nam pla*, which is always served on the side. The other sauce, *nam som*, vinegar with tiny pepper segments floating in it, is for those who won't leave hot enough alone.

And where, you may ask, are the knives? The answer: missing because they're unnecessary. Most Thai food is already cut into small pieces, or at least soft enough to divide with fork or spoon. Thais hold the fork in the left hand and push food with it into the large spoon which, in turn, transfers the morsels to the mouth. Chopsticks are used for certain kinds of food, for instance for picking chunks out of a stew. But if your chopstick technique is shaky don't worry about using fork or spoon instead. Some Thais have trouble with chopsticks, too.

When in Asia...

As a change of taste from Thai cooking, and the coffee-shop version of European food, you can experiment with the cuisines of other Asian countries. By far the most widespread is Chinese food. In Bangkok, you can sample the most important regional schools of Chinese cooking—from Canton, Peking, Shanghai and Szechuan, as well as the less familiar food of the Hakka, Chiu Chow and Hunan people.

Although restaurants specializing in dishes from neighbouring Burma, Laos, Kam-

Girl in school uniform balances bowls in back-street Bangkok restaurant.

puchea and Malaysia are not easy to find in Bangkok, more distant (and better known) cuisines are well represented. Japanese and Korean restaurants, for instance, have proliferated with the tourist trade. For quite different reasons, including the flow of refugees, the number of Vietnamese restaurants has been growing. The significant population of Thais of Indian descent or of Moslem religion explains the ready availability of authentic curries and associated foods.

Western cuisine. Most hotels serve an approximation of European food. For more authenticity you can try the nationality restaurants, often owned by foreign residents. Among the possiblities in Bangkok: American, English, French, German, Hungarian, Italian, Scandinavian and Swiss cooking.

Drinks

Iced water is frequently served at the start of a meal. It's almost bound to be potable in any decent restaurant but if in doubt ask for a bottle of water and skip the ice. Thais usually drink water throughout their meals, postponing tea or coffee until the end. Thai men sometimes drink whisky with dinner. You can drink anything you please and the Thais will not be surprised: juice, soft drink, milk, beer, iced coffee, iced tea or lemonade. (Thai lemonade normally comes salted to fight dehydration in the hot climate; you may not appreciate the taste but it's probably unchangeable.)

All wines are disastrously expensive in Thailand, costing several times the price in the country of origin. Even in a modest restaurant, undistinguished French, German or Portuguese wines often cost more than the whole dinner.

But Thailand produces good beer. The brand names are Singha, Amarit and Kloster, and they're stronger than you think. Weaker and cheaper than you'd think is Thai whisky (Mekhong is the best-known brand).

Streetseller in Pattaya purveys tropical fruits with untranslatable names, but you only have to point.

To Help You Order...

May we have a table?	มีโต๊ะว่างไหม	*Mi tor wang mai?*
I'd like a/an/some...	ฉันอยากจะ	*Chan yak cha...*
beer	เบียร์	*beer*
bread	ขนมปัง	*kha-nome-pung*
coffee	กาแฟ	*kafae*
glass	แก้ว	*kaew*
meat	เนื้อ	*neua*
menu	เมนู	*ma-noo*
milk	นม	*nom*
rice	ข้าว	*kao*
salt	เกลือ	*keua*
soup	ซุป	*soop*
sugar	น้ำตาล	*nam thal*
tea	ชา	*cha*
water	น้ำ	*nam*

...and Read the Menu...

กล้วย	*kluay*	banana
เนื้อ	*neua*	beef
ไก่	*gai*	chicken
ปู	*poo*	crab
แกง	*gaeng*	curry
ไข่	*khai*	egg
ปลา	*pla*	fish
ก๋วยเตี๋ยว	*kwaytio*	noodles
ไข่เจียว	*khai jeow*	omelet
มะละกอ	*ma-la-kor*	papaya
หมู	*moo*	pork
กุ้ง	*gung*	shrimp
แตงโม	*taeng-mo*	watermelon

103

BLUEPRINT for a Perfect Trip

How To Get There

Because of the complexity and variability of the many fares, you should ask the advice of an informed travel agent well before your departure.

BY AIR

Scheduled flights

Bangkok's Don Muang international airport (see also p.108) is the principal gateway to Thailand and a major airport of entry to the East, with services from Europe, the U.S., Canada, Australia and Asia. The flight from London to Bangkok takes approximately 16 hours, from New York 25 hours, from Sydney 12 hours.

Charter flights and package tours

From the U.K. and Eire: A wide range of package tours to Thailand, or tours featuring Thailand as part of a package, are available. Among the most popular is the "fly-cruise": you fly to Bangkok or Singapore, cruising from there to Bali, Jakarta and other Far Eastern ports.

From North America: Several tour operators in the United States offer Group Inclusive Tour (GIT) programmes that feature Bangkok along with other exotic ports of call in the Far East. From 15 to 30 days in length, these tours include air transport from city to city on the itinerary, transfers to and from hotels, hotel accommodation, some sighteeing and the services of an English-speaking guide, some or all meals as well as tips and service charges. These GITs may be extended by four days to include a stop-over in Hawaii.

BY ROAD

Private travel by car to Thailand is for all practical purposes impossible, as the Burmese border is closed.

BY RAIL

From Singapore, trains travel through Malaysia to Bangkok.

105

HOW TO GET THERE

When to Go

Thailand enjoys the best weather of the year just when the northern temperate zone is suffering the worst of winter. November through February are the favoured months in Bangkok, known with irony as the "cool season". The temperature does dip a few degrees below the debilitating heights achieved during the rest of the year, but more important is the lowered humidity. Rain is quite rare.

Although temperatures from 36 to 38 °C (around 100 °F) are common during the hot season, widespread use of air-conditioning relieves the discomfort. The rainy season (monsoon) lasts from about June to October. It rains mostly in the afternoon or evening, cooling and refreshing the tropical air, and inundating the streets.

The following chart gives the average daily temperature and number of rainy days per month in Bangkok:

		J	F	M	A	M	J	J	A	S	O	N	D
average daily	°F	89	91	93	95	93	91	90	90	89	88	87	87
maximum	°C	32	33	34	35	34	33	32	32	32	31	31	31
average daily	°F	68	72	75	77	77	76	76	76	76	75	72	68
minimum	°C	20	22	24	25	25	25	24	24	24	24	22	20
rainy days			2	2	4	5	14	16	19	21	23	17	7	1

CIGARETTES, CIGARS, TOBACCO*. Thai cigarettes, filtered and unfiltered, are sold at kiosks everywhere—by the packet or by the cigarette. Foreign brands, at much higher prices, are offered less openly on the black market. But imported cigars and pipe tobacco are readily available, legally and in great variety. For a novel smoke, try one of the aromatic cigars from northern Thailand, wrapped in young banana leaves; the secret ingredient is dried tamarind seed.

Be careful lighting Thai matches. It's wise to strike them away from you, since they sometimes lose their heads.

A packet of cigarettes, please.	**bu ri nung song**
A box of matches, please.	**mai keet nung klong**
filter-tipped/without filter	**mi kone krong/mai mi kone krong**

CLOTHING. Pack for the tropics, the more cotton the better. A light sweater might come in handy if you're planning a trip to the northern mountains; otherwise, the only place you might need a wrap would be in an excessively air-conditioned restaurant. (Some restaurants have anticipated this and offer a length of cloth as a stole.)

Immodesty must be avoided. Adults do not wear shorts on city streets or when visiting monasteries. Women with plunging necklines will receive plenty of stares, not all admiring. The Thais are strict about covering up, except on the beach, but they are quite casual when it comes to dressing up. Even the Grand Palace no longer requires jackets and ties; almost all restaurants and nightclubs share the informal approach. (It's important to note that an extremely "hippie" look can cause you to be refused entry into Thailand.)

COMMUNICATIONS. For post office opening hours see HOURS section. Branch offices are scattered throughout Bangkok and, for the convenience of visitors, at the Don Muang Airport and major hotels. The main post office is located on New Road near the Oriental Hotel. You'll find large red letter-boxes in the street.

Mail. You can send letters and postcards airmail which arrive within four days to a week in the U.S. or Europe. Surface mail takes at least five weeks. Packages mailed out of the country must be presented for inspection at the Customs Window of the post office and then wrapped in the presence of an inspector. At the wrapping desk your gifts can be prepared for safe shipment.

If you don't know your address in advance, you can have your mail sent to poste restante (general delivery) at the General Post Office. A

Planning Your Budget

To give you an idea of what to expect, here are some average prices in Thai baht (B.). They can only be approximate, however, as inflation takes its toll.

Airport. Limousine service to city centre locations, from international terminal B. 300 (taxi B. 200), from domestic terminal B. 150 (taxi minimally less). Airport departure tax, international flights B. 150, domestic flights B. 20.

Boats. Long-tailed boats and motorized river boats around B. 280 per hour (negotiable), private two-hour canal cruise B. 300–350 per boat.

Buses. City buses B. 2, air-conditioned buses B. 5–15 within city boundary. Air-conditioned coach Bangkok–Pattaya (one way) B. 150 (private operators, pick-up from major hotels). Air-conditioned coach Bangkok–Phuket (one way) B. 299–350 (private operators).

Car hire (international company). *Toyota Corolla 1300/Nissan Sunny 1200* B. 770 per day, B. 5,400 per week with unlimited mileage. *Toyota Corona 1800/Nissan Bluebird* B. 880 per day, B. 6,200 per week with unlimited mileage. *Chauffeur-driven Toyota Crown 2000* B. 220 per hour.

Cigarettes. Local B. 13–15 for a packet of 20, imported B. 30.

Entertainment. Nightclub entry with 2 drinks and floor show B. 150–300.

Guided tours. Floating market morning tour B. 220–300. All-day river excursion to Ayutthaya (with lunch) B. 600–700.

Hairdressers (in top hotels; elsewhere prices considerably lower). *Woman's* haircut B. 320, shampoo and set B. 220. *Man's* haircut B. 100, shave B. 100, shampoo B. 100.

Hotels (air-conditioned double room with bath). Budget B. 900–1,200. Tourist B. 1,200–1,500. First class from B. 1,500. Luxury B. 2,500–4,000. Add 10% service charge and 11% taxes. Rates are for peak months (Dec.–March), and are considerably less at other times.

Massage. B. 200–300 per hour, plus extras.

Meals and drinks. Hotel breakfast B. 265, lunch B. 320, dinner B. 390–500. 10% service charge and 8.25% taxes included. Beer (local) B. 40–90, wine (imported) B. 300–600 per bottle.

Taxis. B. 50–100 in central Bangkok (hotel taxis, twice as much).

Trains. Bangkok–Hat Yai Express: 1st class, one way B. 904, return B. 1,808, 2nd class, one way B. 343, couchette B. 443. Bangkok–Chiang Mai Express: 2nd class couchette (return) B. 770.

An A–Z Summary of Practical Information and Facts

> A star (*) following an entry indicates that relevant prices are to be found on page 107.

A

ADDRESSES. You may wonder at which end to start when you see addresses such as 131 soi Tien Sieng, South Sathorn Road. "Soi" indicates a branch off a main road, so you should look first for the larger road (in this case South Sathorn) and then the lane, alley or smaller road which branches off (here it's Tien Sieng). Remember there may be minor lanes going off these smaller roads, too!

AIRPORTS*. Don Muang international airport (tel. 286-0190/9), north of Bangkok, is Thailand's principal gateway. The arrival and departure terminals are up to the highest international standards. Arriving passengers will find a duty-free shop right in the customs area. Immigration and customs clearances are efficient and swift. In the arrival hall, a full range of facilities, including porters, limousine service, hotel desks and an information bureau of the Tourism Authority of Thailand, is available on a 24-hour basis. Local telephone calls can be made free of charge from call boxes in the arrival and departure halls.

City taxis without yellow plates shoud not be used and are technically illegal. Air-conditioned metro buses pick up at the terminal, but are usually slower if cheaper than limousines. Travel time from the airport to the hotels of Bangkok ranges from 45 minutes to an hour and a half.

Those heading for Pattaya can take an air-conditioned coach there directly from the airport (about a 3-hour trip).

Internal flights. Although long-distance buses and trains are often comfortable, the fast and easy (if expensive) way to get from Bangkok to the far north or south is by air. Domestic airlines run a comprehensive schedule of jet and turboprop flights serving provincial centres from Chiang Rai in the north to Phuket in the west and Hat Yai in the south.

B

BICYCLE and MOPED HIRE. Although most inadvisable in the horror of Bangkok traffic, bikes are for rent to use in the vast Pramane Ground (or Sanam Luang as Thais know it). At beach resorts such as Pattaya and Phuket both bikes and mopeds may be

hired through your hotel reception desk or travel counter; ju[...] ticket for going to distant beaches. An excellent way to expl[...] Chiang Mai is by bike or moped; check with the tourist office.

C

BOAT TRIPS*. Guided tours by excursion boat are a pleasant [...] expensive way to see Bangkok's river and canals. For cheap do-it-you[...] self sight-seeing, take the river-bus (*baht* boat)—only a few baht for a[...] hour's voyage up or down the mighty Chao Phya. For canal explor[...] ations, private long-tailed boats *(hang yao)* may be rented at landings at the end of lanes either side of the Oriental Hotel. Be sure to negotiate the price with the driver in advance. Other canal cruises are available from the landing near the bridge:
2662 New Petchburi Road.

For a wonderful view, try to go just before sunset. See GUIDES AND TOURS.

BUSES*. A well-developed network of city buses serves Bangkok. Fares are very low and service is as good as might be expected in a traffic-jammed metropolis. Though some of the buses are old and cramped, the new air-conditioned models (at a premium fare along special routes) meet high standards. If you plan to cut your expenses by using buses instead of taxis, invest in one of the Bangkok street maps which show the routes. Convenient for tourists is the line that serves the major sights, big hotels, railway stations and shopping centres. All city buses have route numbers marked in arabic numerals but destinations are written in Thai. You don't pay as you enter a city bus; the conductor, jingling a coin box, will come around to sell you a fixed-fare ticket.

Intercity coaches range from rickety veterans to comfortable air-conditioned cruisers. Prices vary accordingly. On the heavily travelled routes, such as Bangkok–Pattaya, luxury coaches of various companies make frequent departures.

Where's the bus stop?   **Pai rod may yu ti nai?**

CAR HIRE*. To rent a car you must be over 21 and hold an international driving licence. You may be asked to pay a deposit equal to the estimated cost of the rental. Larger companies, however, waive this deposit for credit-card holders.

Insurance is not included by most car-hire firms, although one agenc[...] includes insurance when the car is chauffeured by one of their e[...] ployees. Other companies offer insurance on a daily basis at extra co[...] See also DRIVING.

separate poste restante window for cables operates in the telegraph section of the G.P.O. (see below). Always take your passport for identification. You must pay a small service charge for each letter received.

Telegrams. Branch post offices accept telegrams, but for round-the-clock cable and telex service go to the telecommunications department on the ground floor of the General Post Office on New Road.

Telephones. When you call overseas you may have to wait for a dial tone. Overseas calls can be dialled direct or made through the operator (dial 100), by placing them either at the telecommunications department (see above) or through your hotel switchboard. Some hotels add a stiff service charge, even for local calls.

The new street telephones have instructions posted in Thai and English, and the telephone directory comes in an English, as well as Thai, edition. Note that Thai subscribers are listed in alphabetical order by their first names, not their surnames. (Telephone enquiries: 13.)

COMPLAINTS. If you have a dispute with a hotel, merchant or any organization or person in Thailand it's important not to lose your temper. If your complaint has no effect when you try the face-to-face approach, consult the Tourism Authority of Thailand. In serious cases, the Tourist Police can often help to resolve the problem.

CONSULATES and EMBASSIES. Following is a list of consulates, but for a complete one see the yellow pages of the Bangkok telephone directory under "Embassies, Consulates & Legations". In case of Thai visa problems consult any office of the Tourism Authority of Thailand or the government's Immigration Division, telephone 286-9065.

Australia: 37 South Sathorn Rd.; tel. 286-0411; 8 a.m. to 12.30 p.m. and 1.45 to 3 p.m. Monday to Friday.

Canada: Boonmitr Building, 138 Silom Rd., 11th floor; tel. 234-1561; Visa section, 9.30 a.m. to 12 p.m. and 2 to 3.30 p.m. Monday to Friday; other sections, 7 a.m. to 12.30 p.m.

Eire: United Flour Mills Building, 11th floor, 205 Rajawongse Rd.; tel. 223-0876, 223-0470/9.

Japan: 1647 New Petchburi Rd.; tel. 252-6151/9.

New Zealand: 93 Wireless Rd.; tel. 251-8165, 251-8166, 251-8171. **111**

C **United Kingdom:** 1031 N. Wireless Rd.; tel. 252-7161.

U.S.A.: 95 Wireless Rd.; tel. 252-5041–9, ext. 2321; 7.30 a.m. to 12 p.m. Monday to Friday.

CONVERTER CHARTS. Thailand adopted the metric system more than 50 years ago, but a few traditional measures still exist. Of these the most frequently seen: 1 rai = .16 hectare = .4 acre.

Weight

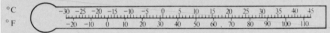

Temperature

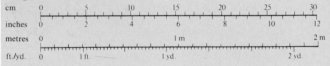

Length

Distance

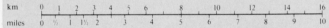

CUSTOMS CONTROLS and ENTRY FORMALITIES. Citizens of most countries need tourist visas to stay more than 15 days in Thailand. For latest regulations check with your travel agent in advance, or ask a Thai consulate. So-called undesirable tourists—meaning presumed "hippies"—may be refused entry, or required to prove financial responsibility. Any visitor may have to prove his solvency by producing the equivalent of 10,000 baht (per person) or 20,000 baht (per family) upon arrival in Thailand (currency, traveller's cheques, credit cards).

Visitors should have certificates proving the validity of their cholera, yellow fever and smallpox vaccinations if they arrive from infected areas. Malaria risk exists in rural areas all over the country. Vaccination against cholera is particularly recommended.

The following chart shows what you may bring into Thailand duty-free, and into your own country when returning home:

Into:	Cigarettes	Cigars	Tobacco	Spirits	Wine
Thailand	200	or 250 g.	or 250 g.	1 l.	or 1 l.
Australia	200	or 250 g.	or 250 g.	1 l.	or 1 l.
Canada	200	and 50	and 900 g.	1.1 l.	or 1.1 l.
Eire	200	or 50	or 250 g.	1 l.	and 1 l.
N. Zealand	200	or 50	or ½ lb.	1 qt.	and 1 qt.
U.K.	200	or 50	or 250 g.	1 l.	and .2 l.
U.S.A.	200	and 100	and *	1 l.	or 1 l.

* a reasonable quantity

There is no restriction on the import of foreign currency, but amounts over the equivalent of $U.S. 10,000 must be declared. On leaving the country you may take out up to $U.S. 10,000 or the equivalent in foreign currency (more if declared). Up to 2,000 baht per person (4,000 baht per family) in Thai currency may be brought in to the country, but no more than 500 baht per person (1,000 baht per family) may be exported. All gold jewellery in your possession must be declared when you arrive, or you risk having it confiscated on departure.

When leaving Thailand note that it's forbidden to export any images of Buddha or other deities. It is also prohibited to export antiquities without special permission from the Fine Arts Department. The shop should be able to handle this for you. Or contact the office directly:

National Museum, Fine Arts Dept., 4 Na Phratatu Road, tel. 222-1831.

DRIVING IN THAILAND. As in many Asian countries, traffic in Thailand is supposed to keep to the left. Driving conditions in the Bangkok metropolis are appalling because of the chronic traffic jams; peak traffic persists almost all day with only brief periods of respite. On the main highways out of town, free-spirited drivers make their own rules. They tend to use whatever part of the road they feel they need, even if it means running another car into a ditch. Losing your temper

D is frowned upon. As you discover the local driving customs—you have few rights, only fears and doubts—you won't need reminding to stay extremely alert. Watch out, too, for buses in one-way streets running in the opposite direction to the traffic. The official speed limit is 40 kilometres per hour in towns, 80 on the highways.

Fuel and oil: Readily available in both regular and super.

Breakdowns: Telephone the rental firm to come and rescue you. In an emergency dial the Highway Police Patrol Centre at 281-6240/41.

Parking: Car-parks and metered parking on some Bangkok streets help to relieve the crush.

Road signs: Many Thai road signs are more or less standard international pictographs. Speed limits are always posted in arabic numerals.

Accident	**u bat hed**
Collision	**rod chon**
Flat tire	**yang bean**
Help!	**chuey duey!**
Police!	**tam ruat!**

DRUGS. Most of the big narcotics arrests in Thailand involve people caught trying to smuggle drugs *out* for sale abroad. Possession of heroin or its variants for trade and distribution is punishable by from five years to life imprisonment (foreigners), death sentence (Thais) and a fine of up to half a million baht. Possessing, trading or smoking marijuana or accessory devices is punishable by as much as six months in prison. Ignorance of Thai law is not a mitigating factor in drug cases.

DRY CLEANING and LAUNDRY. Many hotels return laundry within 24 hours and even within four hours at premium rates. Dry cleaning takes two days unless "express service" is specified (in half the time for 50% extra). Apart from hotels, laundries and dry-cleaning establishments are listed under "Laundries" in the classified telephone directory. There are some semi-self-service launderettes in Thailand.

E **ELECTRICITY.** The standard current in Thailand is 220-volt, 50-cycle A.C.; most hotels have a point for shavers and some have 110-volt sockets also.

EMERGENCIES. The main hospitals treat urgent medical problems 24 hours a day:

Bangkok General Hospital – tel. 314-6771
Bangkok Mission (Adventist) Hospital – tel. 281-1442
Prommitr Hospital – tel. 392-1095/6
Police Hospital, Rajdamri Road – tel. 252-8111

Provincial towns also have fully equipped hospitals. Other numbers which may be useful in an emergency:

Tourist Assistance Centre (Bangkok)	281-0372 or 281-5051
Highway Police Patrol Centre	281-6240/41
Fire	281-6666 or 199
Ambulance	281-1544
All-purpose emergency number	191

GUIDES and TOURS*. The enterprising Bangkok travel trade has devised scores of excursions, from the floating market boat trip to serious archaeological outings. There are eight pages of agencies listed in the classified telephone directory under "Travel Bureaus". For interpreters, see the entry "Translators and Interpreters" in the yellow pages. Avoid unauthorized guides who greet you on the street and offer to show you Bangkok (see TOUTS).

HAIRDRESSERS*. The red-and-white-striped barber's pole denotes both men's and women's hairdressers. The shops in the major hotels generally charge more than others but have two advantages: they are accustomed to dealing with foreign hair, and they probably know a bit of English. In Thailand, even a haircut is a sensuous experience so sit back and enjoy all the attention.

haircut	**tad pom**
shampoo and set	**sa lae set**
blow dry	**pao**
colour rinse	**yorm pom**

HEALTH and MEDICAL CARE. Don't let the heat get you down. If you're unaccustomed to the tropics, respect the midday sun; it can broil you in an hour. To avoid dehydration put plenty of salt on your breakfast eggs. (The Thais put salt in their lemonade.) Spare your digestive system by experimenting gradually until you're more accustomed to the spicy Thai cuisine.

Wear light airy clothing and a hat in the sun. And don't go barefoot (to avoid catching worms).

Check with your doctor before leaving home for his recommendations on malaria prevention. While Bangkok and other principal towns **115**

H are malaria-free, the disease is endemic in some parts of Thailand. See also CUSTOMS CONTROLS AND ENTRY FORMALITIES. Hotels often have doctors on call. Or look in the classified (yellow) pages of the telephone directory under "Physicians & Surgeons MD". For dentists and dental clinics the yellow pages have a section headed "Dentists".

Bangkok has efficient modern hospitals staffed by well-qualified personnel. Since health care can be expensive, your insurance company at home can advise you about a policy covering illness or accident on holiday.

Chemists' shops (pharmacies) are open from about 9 a.m. to 9 p.m., later in some areas. Most foreign drugs are available, though it's wise to check the expiration date on the package.

I need a doctor.	**chan tong karn mo**
I need a dentist.	**chan tong kan mo fan**

HOTELS and ACCOMMODATION*. The equilibrium between hotel supply and demand in Bangkok tends to be delicate, so advance reservations are a very good idea. The capital has more than 12,000 hotel rooms considered suitable for foreign tourists; penny-pinching or adventurous visitors will find many no-frills native-style hotels as well. Of the "suitable" hotels even the cheapest are completely air-conditioned, and almost all have swimming pools and other comforts. At the top end of the scale, in establishments of world-wide repute, guests enjoy every luxury from exemplary architecture and gourmet restaurants to a private zoo or ferry landing.

World-standard hotels are found in the beach resorts and in regional capitals such as Chiang Mai and Hat Yai.

In smaller provincial towns the facilities may be fairly basic—but so are the prices. Find out the room rate and extras in advance: most hotels add tax and service charge to the bill at check-out time.

Youth hostels: Aside from hotel-style accommodation run by youth organizations such as the YMCA, no special facilities exist.

HOURS

Banks: 8.30 a.m. to 3.30 p.m., Monday to Friday.

Department stores: about 10 a.m. to 8 p.m. (usually 10 p.m. in Bangkok), often every day including Sunday.

Government offices: 8.30 a.m. to noon and 1 to 4.30 p.m., Monday to Friday.

Museums: about 9 a.m. to noon and 1 to 4.30 p.m., every day except Monday and Friday in Bangkok; closing days in the provinces are Monday and Tuesday.

Post Offices: Bangkok's main post office 8 a.m. to 8 p.m., Monday to Friday and 8 a.m. to 1 p.m. weekends and holidays. Branch post offices from 8 a.m. to 6 p.m., Monday to Friday and 8 a.m. to 1 p.m. weekends and holidays.

Small shops: early morning until 7 or 8 p.m., often seven days a week.

Telegraph office in General Post Office Building: 24 hours a day, seven days a week.

LANGUAGE. Although English is widely used in hotels and shops—it's the best-known Western language in Thailand—you should try to express some simple phrases in Thai (see below). The Thai language spoken in Bangkok is understood everywhere in the country, though there are many dialects and sub-dialects. In addition, several other languages are widely used, such as Lao in the north-east, Malay in the south, and the Teochiu dialect of Chinese in many different areas. Like Chinese, Thai uses intonation to distinguish between otherwise identical words, making it a very difficult language for foreigners; each syllable can have up to five different meanings depending on how it is "sung". The written language, which looks similar to south Indian script, has 44 consonants plus dozens of vowels, compounds and tone marks. If all this doesn't discourage you, consider Rachasap, a special language used only when speaking to or about Thai royalty!

Try to imitate a Thai to learn how to intone these useful words; your effort will be appreciated by everyone you meet.

General greeting (good morning, afternoon, evening, night, goodbye)	**sawaddi klap** (said by men) **sawaddi ka** (said by women)
Thank you.	**kob khun**
Please.	**ka ru na** (normally understood in context rather than spoken)
Good-bye.	**la gawn** or **sawaddi klap** (said by men) **sawaddi ka** (said by women)

LOST PROPERTY. Check first with your hotel receptionist if you lose anything, then report the loss to the nearest police station or, in Bangkok, to the Tourist Assistance Centre (see TOURIST INFORMATION OFFICES).

117

M **MAPS.** The Tourism Authority of Thailand issues free bus and tourist maps showing the principal attractions of Bangkok. More detailed, commercially produced maps of Bangkok and of Thailand are sold at hotels and bookshops. You can also buy interesting specialized maps of the waterways and markets of Bangkok.

MEETING PEOPLE. Striking up a conversation should be no problem; many Thais welcome the opportunity to practise English. But beware of self-appointed guides and interpreters who accost tourists on the street. They have many ways of costing you money, if only in the added price you'll have to pay a merchant to make up for your guide's secret kick-back. (See also Touts.)

When Thais meet, they greet each other with the "wai", a charming prayer-like gesture full of subtlety. They often try to make foreigners feel more comfortable by shaking hands instead.

Bangkok's free-wheeling nightclub scene should not be confused with real life in Thailand. Men should note that girls who do *not* work in bars and the like tend to be shy, conservative and, in any case, closely supervised by their families.

MONEY MATTERS. The unit of currency in Thailand is the *baht* (abbreviated ฿ or B.), divided into 100 *satang* (pronounced stang). Banknotes come in denominations of 10, 20, 50, 60, 100 and 500 baht. Coins are 25 and 50 satang, 1, 2 and 5 baht. Note that one-baht coins are found in two slightly different sizes (only one can be used in street telephones). A number of tuk-tuks, or minibuses, have been converted into motorized currency-exchange units. They circulate through the streets of central Bangkok, as well as in Pattaya, Phuket and Chiang Mai.

Banks and Money Changers. Normally the exchange rate at banks is the most favourable, and you can cash traveller's cheques or change money there easily. Remember to take along your passport when cashing traveller's cheques. After hours you can change money at your hotel or at shops displaying a sign, in English, "Money Changer".

Although all banks and money changers accept pounds, the American dollar is the surest value when changing money in Thailand; so keep this in mind when buying traveller's cheques or changing money before you leave home. Also, get a good supply of dollar bills—they often smooth out little difficulties and, even in the provinces, are easily convertible.

Credit Cards. Major hotels, restaurants and shops are accustomed to the well-known international charge cards.

Prices. For an idea of what things cost, see the section PLANNING YOUR BUDGET on page 107. Heavier taxes on hotels, restaurants and entertainment make Thailand less of a tourist bargain than in the recent past. And imported goods are always expensive. Still, transport is cheap, especially buses. Thai and Chinese food can be a great bargain, though foreign ingredients, cooking styles and décor raise the price considerably. The worst blow in restaurants is the price of wine. But Thai beer and even the undistinguished local whisky are inexpensive.

Bargaining. Many foreigners feel uncomfortable at it, but bargaining over prices is customary in several areas of Thai life. For instance, taxi fares are negotiated in advance. More protracted bargaining takes place in souvenir shopping and other aspects of commerce; even hotels sometimes have flexible rates. The squeamish can either accept the first price mentioned (which would astound a market trader) or take a fixed-price hotel car to one of the big department stores where the price-tags mean business.

NEWSPAPERS and MAGAZINES. Bangkok has several English-language dailies (*Bangkok Post* and *The Nation*) to complement its big range of Thai and Chinese papers. Newspapers from elsewhere in Asia and Europe are sold at major hotels and bookshops. Magazines and paperback books are also available.

PHOTOGRAPHY. The golden spires, blue skies, green fields and extravagant flowers of Thailand cry out for colour film. Standard brands and sizes of film are easily available. You can have your pictures processed in one hour (express service) or five hours (standard service). Exposed film can also be sent home at "small package" rates.

A special show—classical dancing, sword-fighting and Thai boxing—is staged for photographers on Thursday and Sunday mornings at the Oriental Hotel. There are many other opportunities for filming these distinctive pageants but never under such perfect conditions.

One caution: Resist any temptation to take trick pictures of Buddha statues and other religious objects, or even isolated, dilapidated archaeological relics. For instance, never pose anyone touching such a statue. Outraged Thais might accuse you of gross disrespect, however unintended. You should check with your guide if you intend to take pictures in temples or other religious places.

P **POLICE.** A special force of Thai Tourist Police operates in crucial areas of Bangkok—near tourist attractions and major hotels. More than 100 officers, linguists all, stand ready to protect or advise foreigners. They wear the beige military-style uniform of ordinary Thai police with "Tourist Police" shoulder patches.

PUBLIC HOLIDAYS. Since many Thai holidays are fixed to the lunar calendar, the dates vary from year to year. Banks and government offices close on these days, but daily life is not necessarily disrupted. The only notable exception to this is for the Chinese New Year, not a public holiday in Thailand, but a time when most commerce closes down. See also TIME AND CALENDAR DIFFERENCES.

January 1	New Year's Day
May 1	Labour Day
May 5	Coronation Day
August 12	H.M. Queen's Birthday
October 23	Chulalongkorn Day, honouring Rama V
December 5	H.M. King's Birthday and National Day
December 10	Constitution Day
December 31	New Year's Eve (partly observed)
Movable dates	Chinese New Year (partly observed)
	Maka Puja. Commemoration of meeting at which the Buddha preached the central doctrines of Buddhism
	Chakri Day, honouring Rama I
	Songkran Day, Water Festival, formerly Thai New Year
	Visakha Puja. Commemoration of the Buddha's birth, enlightenment and death
	Asalaha Puja. Commemoration of the first sermon of the Buddha
	Khao Phansa, first day of Buddhist Lent

R **RADIO and TV.** Four Bangkok TV channels broadcast in colour and black-and-white. Many programmes are foreign shows, mostly American, dubbed into Thai. In deference to tourists, the foreign colony and students of foreign languages, the original sound track is broadcast simultaneously over FM radio. Most hotels with TV sets provide a choice of sound channels.

The Thai national radio service broadcasts English programmes early and late in the morning daily on 97 mHz FM and 920 kHz AM. Short-wave programmes of the BBC and Voice of America are best received morning or night.

RELIGIOUS SERVICES. In Thailand 93% of the population are Theravada Buddhists, but Moslem, Christian, Hindu and other faiths are well represented. For foreign visitors, Protestant and Catholic services in Bangkok are advertised in Saturday's editions of the *Bangkok Post*. A more complete listing may be found under "Churches" in the classified telephone directory.

TABOOS and CUSTOMS. Ignorance of Thai sensibilities can cause much embarrassment. The monarchy is greatly revered, so the slightest indication of disrespect, even accidental, could have serious consequences. This even applies to money bearing the king's likeness.

Religion plays a most important part in the life of the Thais. When you visit a temple, dress soberly—no shorts or revealing blouses. Wear shoes, but you must remove them before entering the chapel. Never show disrespect to a religious object or to Buddhist monks and nuns (don't offer money to a monk, but you can offer a cigarette). You should not discuss politics with monks, although you may talk of your country and religion. Women are not allowed in certain temples nor should they touch monks or novices.

Note that the head is considered sacred so you must not touch anyone there. Don't point your feet toward's another's body (remember this especially in temples, where you'll see worshippers' feet tucked behind them), nor use them to open a door. Don't lose your temper or display strong emotion (including boisterous thanks). Finally, in spite of Bangkok's reputation, public displays of affection between the sexes (including hand-holding) are just "not done".

TAXIS* and SAMLORS. In Bangkok you don't have to whistle for a taxi. Just look at one and the driver will jam on the brakes. Taxis are so plentiful that they can be a nuisance. Drivers congregate near hotels and cruise alongside strolling foreigners to solicit business.

Almost all Bangkok taxis have meters, some of them apparently in working order—but they are virtually never used. You must haggle over the fare before you enter the cab. Once agreed, the price is a matter of honour; no tip is expected. For fewer frustrations ask your hotel receptionist to write your destination in Thai so you can show it to the driver, as foreigners' pronunciation of street or place names is rarely

T understood. While you're at it, ask the clerk what an appropriate fare should be. It depends on distance and the amount of traffic.

If you can't stand the haggling and the language problem you can take an air-conditioned hotel taxi. The fares are posted; they are usually at least twice what a public taxi would ask. The drivers often know some English.

Some good-sized provincial towns have no conventional taxis at all. You can take a samlor (see below) or, for longer trips, hail an empty minibus. In either case, be sure you agree on the fare in advance.

Samlors/Tuk-Tuks: These noisy little vehicles nip in and out of the Bangkok traffic. Samlors cost a few baht less than four-wheeled taxis, always subject to negotiation before you sit down. Useful, and adventurous, for short trips.

THEFT. Beware of pickpockets in crowded market-places. Purse-snatchers, now motorized in Bangkok, escape on a motorbike almost before the victim realizes that a crime has been committed. Don't tempt bandits by flaunting jewels or ostentatious clothes. Never leave anything irreplaceable in your hotel room; take advantage of the safety deposit box. At seaside resorts never leave any valuables on the beach when you go swimming. At Phuket the authorities further advise tourists to avoid isolated beaches, where they might be accosted by itinerant robbers.

TIME AND CALENDAR DIFFERENCES. Although Thailand has officially adopted the Western 12-month calendar, the traditional lunar calendar is used for ceremonies and everyday activities. Major festivals usually fall on a full moon period. Another difference: dates are calculated from the year Buddha was born (543 B.C.). For instance, the year 2523 B.E. (Buddhist Era) in Thailand corresponded to our year 1980.

Thailand time year-round is GMT plus 7 hours. The following chart shows the time in January in some selected cities. In March/April, when British and U.S. clocks advance one hour, Thailand stays the same.

New York	London	**Bangkok**	Sydney
midnight	5 a.m.	**noon**	4 p.m.

TIPPING. In simple native-style restaurants and snack bars tipping is not customary. It is better to tip nothing at all than to leave a one-baht tip, which is considered an insult. Taxi drivers are normally not tipped. Further guidelines:

Barber	15%
Hairdresser	10%
Hotel maid, per week	B. 50 (optional)
Lavatory attendant	B. 5
Porter	B. 10
Tourist guide	15% (optional)
Waiter	10%

TOILETS. Try to find a hotel or restaurant. In luxury establishments the lavatory may be attended, in which case a tip is appropriate. Up-country you will encounter Eastern-style toilets-in-the-floor. In places without running water you will always find a huge jar of water nearby. Scoop water out for flushing and washing.

Where are the toilets?   **hong nam yu ti nai?**

TOURIST INFORMATION OFFICES. The Tourism Authority of Thailand operates an information stand in the arrivals hall of Bangkok's international airport. You can also obtain leaflets, maps and advice on the main floor of the T.A.T.'s head office:

Ratchadamnoen Nok Ave., near the Ratchadamnoen Boxing Stadium, Bangkok 10100; tel: 282-1143 / 7.

At the same address you'll find the Tourist Assistance Centre which can provide help in all situations. Call 281-5051 or 281-0372 day and night.

Branch offices of T.A.T. at Chiang Mai, Kanchanaburi, Nakhon Ratchasima (Korat), Pattaya, Hat Yai and Phuket have regional information and maps. In Chiang Mai their address is:
135 Praisani Road; tel. 235-334.

Overseas addresses of the Tourism Authority of Thailand:

Australia: 12th floor, Royal Exchange Bldg., Pitt and Bridge St., Sydney N.S.W. 200; tel. 27 75 40.

T **Japan:** Hibiya Mitsui Bldg., 1–2, Yurakucho 1-Chome, Chiyoda-ku, Tokyo 100; tel. (03) 580-6776/7.

United Kingdom: 9 Stafford St. (corner Albermarle St.), London W1X 3FE; tel. 499-7679, 499-7670.

U.S.A.: 5 World Trade Center, Suite 2449, New York, N.Y. 10048; tel. (212) 432-0433.
510 West 6th St., Suite 1212, Los Angeles, CA 90014; tel. (213) 627-0386.

TOUTS. In Bangkok, and to a lesser extent in the big provincial towns, the tourist is often pestered by touts, black marketeers and pimps. Some are charmingly convincing, others obnoxiously persistent. The best course is to smile and walk away. If you want a bona fide guide, ask a travel agency. If you need advice about shopping, ask the Tourism Authority of Thailand for their "Official Shopping Guide" booklet. And as for pimps, in Thailand they are superfluous.

TRAINS *(rod fai).* Although the competing air-conditioned buses often go faster, Thailand's state railway system provides an efficient means of seeing the country. A train is, after all, an adventure, no less so in a crowd of friendly Thai travellers. There are reasonably luxurious, air-conditioned first-class cars, comfortable second-class accommodation (including couchettes to reserve) and old-fashioned dining cars. Travel agents, hotel desks and the information office at the main (Hualompong) railway station can tell you about schedules and fares.
Bangkok's three main stations are Hualompong on Rama IV Road (for the north and north-east, and for express trains to the south), Makkasan on Nikom Makkasan Road (for the east) and Thonburi on Bangkok Noi, Rod Fai Road (for slower trains to the south). Call 223-7010/20 for general information on rail travel.

W **WATER.** Don't drink the tap water in Thailand. Most hotels place a bottle or flask of purified water in every room. Responsible restaurants serve bottled water and pure ice, but be cautious about the ice in drinks at roadside stands. To be on the safe side in questionable situations, you can insist on bottled water or soft drinks and beer without ice.

124   A bottle of drinking water.   **nam dum nung khuad**

SOME USEFUL EXPRESSIONS

yes/no	**chai/mai chai**
please/thank you	**ka ru na/kob khun**
excuse me	**kho tot**
you're welcome	**mai pen rai**
where/when/how	**ti nai/mua rai/yang rai**
how long/how far	**nan tao rai/klai khae nai**
yesterday/today/tomorrow	**mua wan ni/wan ni/prung ni**
day/week/month/year	**wan/sap da/duan/pi**
left/right	**sai/khwa**
up/down	**bon/lang**
good/bad	**di/mai di**
big/small	**yai/lek**
cheap/expensive	**mai paeng/paeng**
hot/cold	**run/yen**
old/new	**kao/mai**
open/closed	**poed/pid**
Does anyone here speak English?	**ti ni mi kai pud pa sa ang-kid yipun dai mai?**
I don't understand.	**chan mai kao chai**
Please write it down.	**karuna khien**
Help me.	**chuey duey**
Get a doctor, quickly.	**darm mo reo**
What time is it?	**khi mong?**
I'd like…	**chan tong karn…**
How much is that?	**raka tao rai?**
Waiter!/Waitress!	**khun klap** (said by men) **khun ka** (said by women)

NUMBERS

one	**neung**	eight	**pat**
two	**song**	nine	**kow**
three	**sam**	ten	**sip**
four	**si**	eleven	**sip-et**
five	**ha**	twelve	**sip-song**
six	**hok**	twenty	**yi-sip**
seven	**chet**	thirty	**sam-sip**

Index

An asterisk (*) next to a page number indicates a map reference.